the Question Corner

Family values spoken here!

JERRY STEPHENS

There are many Church laws and regulations that govern Catholic lives and faith journeys. Most are well defined, in force to raise spiritual awareness as well as preventing dissent. Still, written laws don't always account for the human aspect, the gentle love and concern that brought Jesus into the world to offer us forgiveness and salvation. I will try to answer these questions in a way that presents official church policy.

Still, though, I remain concerned that compassion and understanding are sometimes a missing element in regulations, and will also try to visualize what I think Jesus Himself might have felt and answered.

ISBN-13: 978-1500968762
ISBN 10: 1500968765

Know more - participate more - believe deeper!

DEDICATION

My deepest thanks to my wife, Darlene, for her support

and help. and also for our 51 years (and counting)

of a wonderful marriage.

Her steadfast faith nourishes my own,

CONTENTS

NOTES

Religion can be annoyingly complex, and yet is also surprisingly simple. It consists of acceptance and respect for a creator. Passion rules us when we talk about things that are deeply felt. The things we love, hate or embrace – politics, relationships, and – yes – religion, can provoke stormy seas. Why? I love my vision of God and church, and I hope you love yours as well. God made us caring people, yet there has been more violence, death and hatred arising from the various nuances of religion than any other thing in the universe! So I ask that you bear with me as I share my thoughts and perspective, and hope that a few my ideas remain in memory somewhere even when I have gone on to eternity.

Most of these questions and answers were collected during 7 years of teaching the Rite of Christian Initiation for Adults in a local Catholic parish. The answers do not necessarily reflect official views of Catholic authorities or theologians, but certainly have value in helping us better understand a wonderful religion, rich in history, though complex almost beyond belief.

If additional information is needed please seek deeper resources or consult your local priest.

CHAPTER A - SACRAMENTS

A-1 Question: People talk about the "mystery" of the Holy Eucharist, or the "paschal mystery". I've never really understood what they're talking about – do you?

Answer: You are so right! Sometimes we take for granted that others are tuned into all things Catholic, and understand terms, practices or beliefs that might be confusing if not properly explained. I've tried to cover many of these before, but please keep the questions coming about things that may be stumping you.

The "**mystery**" of the Eucharist is simply that – though the bread and wine of consecration seem unchanged in all physical ways - we know through faith that they have actually been changed into the body and blood of Christ. The "accidents" (the appearance) remains unchanged, but the "substance" becomes sacred and divine. There is a Church word to describe the event – transubstantiation. Whew! Lots of syllables.

This is a central, core belief of Catholicism. We can't understand through our senses that this has happened, but only through our trust in the words of God, and faith in Jesus. Thus, the "mystery".

The "**paschal mystery**" refers to the entire passion, death and resurrection of Christ, and how this wondrous succession of events allows us to participate in the salvation they have won for all. The paschal mystery is celebrated through Baptism, Easter and each sacrament that brings us to into the life of Christ. The word "pasch" is a Jewish term for the Passover, in which the angel of death "passed-over" Jewish homes without causing harm, while destroying Egyptian first-born children. This God-imposed punishment won freedom from slavery for the captive Hebrews, and is still celebrated.

Jesus, we see that the Hebrew nation rejected your instructions, and we hope we might have learned from their difficulties, trying to make sure that You are the very pinnacle of our lives, our obligations and our love.

A-2 QUESTION: I've seen Catholics take communion in non-Catholic services. Is this allowed, or can non-Catholics receive the Eucharist during our mass?

ANSWER: Sorry, but no. The central pillar of belief for Catholics is that the Eucharist is the actual body and blood of Christ, and we guard that sacred presence very carefully. For Catholics to attend a communion where the bread and wine are felt to be simply symbolic would give a false impression that we regard our Eucharist the same way, or that we don't see any difference between faiths. Feel free to attend non-Catholic services on special occasions when your presence won't scandalize the members, such as a friend's wedding or funeral – but please don't partake during the "communion" service.

As for non-Catholics who happen to attend mass, we hope that they refrain from taking the Eucharist out of respect for our beliefs. The prayer books in the pews mention this, and – in cases such as weddings or funerals when many attendees are from other faiths, the celebrant will often say something like, "While we respect good people of all faiths, and look forward eagerly to a day when we can be re-united in our belief, we haven't yet fully achieved that unity. For those present who are of another faith, we would love to have you come forward for a blessing during the communion service, indicating such by crossing your arms, but would ask that the blessed Eucharistic bread and wine be taken only by fully initiated Catholics." These responses have been scripted by and according to Canon 844-4, and through the Guidelines For the Reception of Communion, as published by the National Council of Catholic Bishops.

There are some in the Church hierarchy who feel that Christ would want sinners, the damaged and the unconverted to join in the healing of being nourished by a sacred meal when God's family meets at mass. Such compassion is understandable and perhaps laudable, but definitely is in contradiction with the published norms.

My God, I look forward to the day when all of your widespread family may worship as one, partake as one, unite as one, and eventually come before you having earned the right to spend eternity in Your presence.

A-3 QUESTION: Why do Catholics keep going to confession as if they aren't already saved? Don't you know Christ died so anyone who truly believes in Him is saved simply through His sacrifice?

ANSWER: Yes, I thank God every day for allowing Jesus to purchase my salvation through His sacrifice. I believe He offers me that gift, but only if I can live in accordance with His will. I often deal with other faith leaders in my work, and had this same conversation recently with a pastor of a fairly mainstream protestant faith. He said, "Even your Pope goes to confession once a week. Why? Haven't you been born again, and accepted Jesus? If so, you'd know you were already saved!"

(It's pretty neat to have friendly, productive discussions with other faiths. What a way to discover the tremendous pool of belief we hold in common, and learn respect for each other!)

Anyhow, I asked him about the other side to the "salvation" coin – our built-in gift of free will! Jesus certainly won our salvation, and opened Heaven to believers, but we have to reach out and embrace that offering. And keep embracing - and keep embracing. Through our free will, we can always reject or walk away from our spiritual inheritance through sin. I asked the pastor if one of his "born again" parishioners decided to become a mass murderer later in life – was he still automatically entitled to salvation? Sorry, but I don't think so! Sure, God leaves the offer on the table, but we have to do our part by earning a right to the prize. Through confession and repentance, though, we can always take those few steps back to where Jesus is waiting with open arms and a warm welcome! Wow, what a deal!

Well, I don't know if we ended up in complete agreement, but that pastor did admit he'd do some serious re-thinking about automatically and permanently winning salvation just by accepting Christ. Well, see you in church – time for that periodic soul-dusting-off we call the Sacrament of Reconciliation! I've got some salvation to protect!

Thank you my God for knowing that in my weakness I will need Your guidance and Your forgiveness throughout my life. You know all there is to know of me, yet your love continues. Have patience with my disobedience and my failures, that my faith and life may eventually bring me to your arms.

A-4 QUESTION: Is Baptism or Confession the only sacrament that forgives sin?

ANSWER: Oh, heck no! The Sacrament of the Sick certainly serves the same function, and even receiving the Eucharist can and does forgive minor sin under the right conditions. You must have an inward sorrow for sin, pray for forgiveness and pledge to try to avoid these sins again. *A person conscious of serious sin, however, should first be cleansed through the Sacrament of Reconciliation.* (Catechism of the Catholic Church CCC1393) I'm reminded, too, that as we walk forward to receive the Body and Blood of Christ, we are walking away from all of our weaknesses, sorrows, errors and mistakes – going joyfully to join with our God. We return to our seats cleansed and purified. Remember this as you join the communion line, and feel the freedom of leaving the gunk and junk back behind you in the pew.

Think of this, "I have been cleansed and forgiven. I have been nourished at God's own table. I have rid myself of anything that displeases Him, and this day is good, and I am good."

A-5 Question: How often can I receive Holy Communion?

Answer: The Church encourages reception of the Eucharist as often as possible, even daily. We are, of course, required to receive it a minimum of once each year, usually within the Easter Season, properly prepared and cleansed by the sacrament of Reconciliation. (ccc 1389) If the question is "*Can I receive more than once a day*?", the answer is - yes. Assuming you are part of a Eucharistic liturgy, especially the mass, and are not just seeking a multiple communion for its own sake, you may receive a second time the same day – for instance, at a morning mass, and later at a funeral or wedding. Though not specified in the Catechism, you'll find the provision in the 1983 Code of Canon Law - *"Canon 917: One who has received the Blessed Eucharist may receive it a second time on the same day only within a Eucharistic celebration in which that person participates.*

What a great privilege you allow me, Jesus, to come to your table repeatedly, to nourish my soul, to fill me with your strength, and to unite with others around the world in giving you praise and worship.

A-6 Question: What do you think about taking Communion in the hand, standing up?

Answer: You're asking somebody from the old school, who served maybe 10,000 Latin masses and received communion on the tongue at an altar rail more times than you could count! For many who were raised that way, it can seem irreverent to receive standing up, let alone taking it in our own sweaty hands. Appendix I of the General Instructions of the Roman Missal state, "The practice must remain the option of the communicant. The priest or minister of Communion does not make the decision as to the manner of reception of Communion." Me, though – I love having that option! It always boils down to our reverence for and love of the Eucharist – the true presence of Christ. Church rules change with the times, and rightly so. In previous centuries it has been very common to receive standing up, or – to go back to the beginning - lying at leisure during a Sabbath meal. We don't need to get so rooted in the methods of receiving that we forget the reason for the sacrament itself – to join joyfully and fully with Jesus by taking His Body and Blood. He begs us to come to the table to receive cleansing and strengthening. As it flows from His hand into our hand or mouth, standing or kneeling – it is a great gift!

Lord, help me to see and experience You deeply each time I take your Body and Blood at communion; to know that I receive the sacred and sublime, and that I am as privileged as one of Your apostles as I join them at the table of your love. Nourish and strengthen me, my God.

A-7 Question: Why do Catholics have to confess to priests instead of repenting at public altar calls as many faiths do? Why do you call that practice by several different names, anyway?

Answer: Well, we face our confessors directly for several reasons, though mainly because Jesus gave instructions to His apostles during what is usually called the Great Commissioning that "*If you forgive the sins of any, their sins have been forgiven them. If you retain the sins of any, they have been retained.*" (John 20:21-23). Those same apostles took their charge very seriously, and eventually passed those same instructions to their successors – the priests and bishops.

You might also note that "Reconciliation Rooms" normally offer screens behind which persons seeking forgiveness may remain anonymous if desired.

When the priest feels that our repentance is real and in the name of Jesus absolves us from our sins, we know they're gone! This relief gives Catholics a great deal of peace and confidence in salvation. As a whole, we need the help of shrinks much less than the general population. Yes, it can sometimes be difficult to speak your faults to a priest, but that is part of repentance. They are never judgmental, often able to counsel with good advice, never share a confidence and are wonderfully patient and understanding. We feel the Sacrament of Reconciliation should be used fairly often or whenever we sink into serious sin. The Church also requires that we do so at least once a year. Salvation has indeed been won by Jesus, but we can reject the offering by walking away in sin. What a relief to come back to God!

The different names we use for the sacrament reflect the ways in which it acts. It was in past years commonly referred to as

"Confession", since that is exactly what we do. It is also known as the "Sacrament of Penance", since the priest normally imposes some small symbolic penance to help us show God we are sorry for having strayed. This wonderful sacrament is now called, much more accurately, as the "Sacrament of Reconciliation", since through it we are forgiven, reconciled to God, and once again made full partners in salvation.

May I always seek you when my heart is heavy, and especially when the burden of my own sins is overpowering. I know that forgiveness is always available to me, and that I can lay down my guilt at any time I seek you in repentance.

A-8 Question: (from a parishioner) I recently attended a wedding between a Catholic and a non-Catholic, presided over by a priest. While beautiful, it was just held in a public hall, without a mass. Is this a valid marriage?

ANSWER: Well, we certainly send the happy couple our best! Yes, the marriage is undoubtedly valid civilly and is also sacramental in nature, as it was witnessed by a religious officiator. However, Catholic marriage rules are complicated for good reason, and might have been shortcut, perhaps resulting in a union with problems. We want Catholic marriages to be rock-solid, so we offer counseling, Pre-Cana classes, and seek agreements from the non-Catholic partner about how the children will be allowed a religious upbringing. We also make certain each partner understands the difficulties that will arise in any union; that there is nothing like an existing pregnancy putting pressure on the two, or a shotgun hanging from anybody's hand. We talk to them about their duties and responsibilities to each other and to the offspring, and make sure that they are of age and mentally mature enough to enter a sacred union. There shouldn't be hidden reservations, agendas, or unshared physical or dependency problems. A sacramental marriage involves a verbal contract between the bride and groom… and God, with the priest as principal witness. We feel that such a contract is for life, not to be broken or set aside.

Now – if all this was done, as well as seeking permission from the local Bishop to enter a mixed marriage, and to have the liturgy somewhere other than a church building – then we're all in good shape. Hopefully, the priest officiator covered all the bases adequately. Otherwise - underlying weaknesses could develop into eventual failure, and even to perhaps serve as a basis for an annulment, which the Church always hopes to avoid.

Hopefully, this explains briefly about 20 pages of Canon Law, but always feel free to seek advice from your local priest, marriage coordinator, or diocesan tribunal. God Bless!

Jesus, may you make of this marriage a sacred feast, a blessed union, a fruitful and loving family, an enduring relationship, a nurturing home.

A-9 Question: I've been asked to be a Baptismal sponsor. Why is it necessary for me to be confirmed before I can become a godparent?

Answer: Becoming a godparent is a much more serious obligation than we sometimes realize. It means that you accept full responsibility for the spiritual growth and instruction in Catholicism of that baby, if the family fails to provide it. It means that you will remain available to answer questions and try to guide the child all through its life, so that the boy or girl will come to God's salvation eventually. The Church understands that a person who hasn't gotten far enough in their own spiritual development to receive the full complement of sacraments of initiation – Baptism, Reconciliation,

Eucharist and Confirmation – might be more apt to fail in their god-parental duties than somebody who has "gone the course". There is no desire to keep you from being a godparent – simply an effort being made to ensure that the best spiritual interests of the child are protected. At least one godparent must be fully initiated, so you might think about joining the RCIA or the adult Confirmation classes. God bless you for your willingness to stand up for the newborn!

My Lord, there is so much I don't know about your wondrous religion, yet I am comforted that I only need to find You in my heart and in my life to become the person you have always wanted me to be. Help and bless me as you will.

A-10 Question: Just what is this "Eucharist" we keep hearing about?

Answer: The core belief of the Catholic Church revolves around the very real presence of Jesus Christ in the form of consecrated bread and wine, which becomes His Body and Blood. The Greek word for this wonderful gift of divine presence is "Eucharist". The liturgy of the Mass reenacts Christ's actions during the Last Supper, as He stated, *" Take this, all of you, and eat it: this is my body which will be given up for you."* In the same way, He took the cup, filled with wine. He gave you thanks, and giving the cup to his disciples, said: "*Take this, all of you, and drink from it: this is the cup of my blood, the blood of the new and everlasting covenant. It will be shed for you and for all so that sins may be forgiven. DO THIS IN MEMORY OF ME."* (see also Luke 14: 17-20, and John 6: 35-40, and 48-58) Ever since that moment, the Apostles and each succeeding generation has celebrated Christ's triumph by repeating a Eucharistic consecration and by consuming the Body and Blood of our savior. We, in essence, join the Apostles themselves as they enjoy a sacred meal from God's table. What a wonderful privilege we possess!

You have not died in vain, my gentle and loving Jesus! Your sacrifice continues to enlighten, inspire and comfort. Hold my hand as I approach your table, as I am overwhelmed by the sacredness I dare to come toward.

A-11 Question: I just heard a radio preacher blast Christians who were baptized as babies, saying they were "unsaved, living in spiritual darkness of the soul." What the heck does he mean?

Answer: Probably not enough room here, but that particular issue has raged for years. Evangelical, fundamentalist Christian denominations believe it takes a deliberate and informed adult effort to accept Christ personally "as Lord and Savior", to confess wrongdoing publicly, and receive a "baptism of the Holy Spirit." This then guarantees them salvation, regardless of behavior later in life. This is not Christianity as preached by Jesus and the Apostles. Doesn't make sense to me! I've met a few "christians" who don't act or appear to be the ideal "saved" person, and you probably have also.

The Sacrament of Confirmation fortifies our Baptism, trusting the Holy Spirit to continue giving us the strength and grace to succeed in finding salvation.. We instead have come to rely on God's love, mercy and wisdom to handle these tender souls with compassion.

Through baptism, we ask the Holy Spirit to remove original sin, and to grant us strength to resist Satan. We know that baptism marks a person spiritually as a member of

God's family – but it <u>does not</u> automatically make them "saved". All of us must struggle to live a life in obedience to God's will to find eternal salvation, which is only offered to us through the sacrifice of Jesus. We can all, regardless of our baptism, lose our way to the pearly gates by making poor choices. We have the gift of free will, allowing us to become worthy of salvation or to reject it.

There is a ton of evidence that the Apostles practiced infant baptism, a genuine *baptism of the Spirit,* (instead of a baptism of *repentance* as given by John) from the earliest days of Christianity. Peter's very first sermon, the day of Pentecost, said, *"Repent and let each of you be baptized in the name of Jesus Christ for the forgiveness of your sins; and you shall receive the gift of the Holy Spirit. For the promise is for you <u>and your children,</u>.....)* (Acts 2:38-39) Many other references report baptism given to whole households, and all the earliest historians of the Church acknowledge infant baptism.

The Catholic Church has <u>always</u> recommended the baptism of children. Trust in history. Trust in the wisdom of your Church. But... always realize that while your baptism indeed marks you as a child of God, it is up to you to accept – by your lifestyle – the salvation Christ has offered you. May God bless!

By this baptism was I made a child of God, and I carry the mark of His love deeply on my soul. May my every thought and action reflect, then, the face of God as the lifeblood of the divine has altered me forever.

A-12 <u>Question</u>: From an email ...Hi, yes, I have fallen away from my Catholic home church for about 3 years. I did this because I was confused why Catholics baptize babies without having sin yet. I know about the fallen sin of Adam and Eve. However, babies have no acknowledgement of sin. When one becomes aware of sin, then I believe immersion of full body and head baptism, not just sprinkles of water. Actually, how Jesus left the example for us. Please explain why the Catholic Church does this, and do you think the church might change baptisms to when one is old enough to choose to be immersed?

Thank you, Your sister in Christ

ANSWER: To: My sister in Christ…

I received your email, and am very glad to hear from you. As the email is the only contact I have for now, I'll try to hit some high notes in answer to your question. Maybe we'll have a chance to talk sometime soon.

Infant baptism - how that has been such a pain in the side of so many! In Jesus' day there was only a baptism of repentance, such as John was administering in the Jordan. Christ, of course, brought the idea of Baptism of the Holy Spirit - an infusion of God's very being into the person receiving the baptism. There are a couple of catch-phrases I like to keep around to remind myself of the basics. *WWJD - What Would Jesus Do?* When I have questions, I try to put myself there, in the Creator's place (as much as is possible, anyway) and I find a compassion, a love, a desire to be there present to and for sinners, the weak, the sick and the misguided. Jesus didn't want to be with the big shots, just those people who really needed to hear his message - people like me. And I am comforted, and can perceive at least a little, how He might view my questions.

The other thing I try to keep in mind is, "*How would the 12 Apostles have answered the question. What did they teach at the time - the best informed people in the early church?*" All of them taught then, and throughout their lives, that baptism belonged to all people they encountered. Mostly adults, of course - but in many, many cases - to whole families, both Jew and Gentile. Crowds that numbered in the thousands, men, women and children. Baptism does forgive sins if they exist, of course. I've taught many adults in the RCIA, and known their excitement when they are filled with the Spirit. They usually receive baptism the most symbolically intense way - by immersion if possible. If not in whole, then waist deep at least with a gallon of water poured over their head. Yet the Apostles simply taught that any moving water, "living water" symbolically brought life to those who received it. Original Sin, in my opinion is simply a lack of something, not an actual black mark on someone's soul, but a lack of God's light. When baptism is received - the one time in life it may be administered - that soul is marked forever as a "child of God", and the void of original sin is displaced with wondrous newness.

No, of course infants haven't sinned. Is reaching the age of reason before receiving the sacrament more meaningful, more complete? But the purpose is not only to forgive, but in their case especially more to change and become someone complete in God's love and care. We have precedents of infant baptism all through the early church, including those first 12 bishops. People were baptized wherever and whenever - in rivers, lakes and ponds if possible - in garden fountains and while sitting at table. Moving water - signifying a washing away - a dying to an old life - rising from that symbolic dying into a new life in God, and - of course - repeating the words written in the Gospels. *I baptize you in the name of the Father, and of the Son, and of the Holy Spirit.*

When adults are baptized I am excited - knowing that everything in their past has been taken away and forgotten – (if they receive it in the spirit of faith and truth) - they are now an entirely new being, at least spiritually. I believe the same for babies and children below the age of reason - but that is only one small aspect of Christianity. Catholicism is such a wonderful religion, and to deliberately throw it away for one confusing thing is very sad. People leave the faith for many reasons, but often return as they mature in spirituality. It seems to occur mostly to those who thought about it, questioned it, and decided to step away for a while. Most return eventually, because they are usually our very best - not simply followers.

You would also be aware of the other sacraments of initiation - Reconciliation, First Eucharist and Confirmation. The Church teaches that Confirmation echoes the Pentecostal reception of the Holy Spirit. Most faiths have a coming-of-age ceremony, celebrating when callow children become youth old enough to have adult perception. This, again the church teaches, is basically the second half of baptism. That young soul was dedicated to God - made an actual member of God's family - through his/her baptism. Now, at Confirmation, the Holy Spirit is asked to come to them, instruct them, give them strength of purpose and conviction, to fulfill them spiritually. Adult converts usually receive both sacraments sequentially.

There was always a concern in the early Church that babies who had not been dedicated to God would be lost. A concept called Limbo became popular, where deceased babies went to be comfortable, but less than they would have experienced in Heaven. Thank goodness that picture has been discarded. Now we leave their fate to the tender and compassionate mercy of God. Why would He, who created everyone perfectly and who loves each of them perfectly, commit those young souls to something less than perfection? So, now infant baptism no longer has some of the urgency it had for centuries, but is still practiced, as it has been since the very beginning of Christianity. Don't let one thing discourage you away from Catholicism. The basic beliefs, theology and structures initiated by Jesus and the Apostles still hold the whole structure together today. There are always things that have been instituted by men that can be questioned, but most of those things are simply the dressings that adorn the basics - the liturgies, the "bells and smells". I know that many non-Catholic faith expressions find fault with many things we do, or with what they think (often mistakenly) that we believe. Don't let them bring confusion to your faith life.

May God in His wisdom bless you with an inquiring mind and heart!

A-13 Question; I'm a divorced Catholic. Am I really banned from receiving the sacraments?

Answer: It's tragic that many divorced Catholics no longer feel part of the Church, or feel they can't participate in the sacraments. Civil divorce is fully understood by the Church, and sometimes even encouraged in cases like spousal abuse, danger to the children, etc. This is often the only way to assure property division, parental rights, who gets Aunt Mabel's silver and who gets Rover. BUT ... while the Church sometimes acknowledges that divorce is a legal necessity, a true Christian marriage is never actually dissolved in the process. Marriage vows taken between two mature, unpressured adults and that third person... God... in a religious setting, witnessed by a priest or minister, are as unbreakable as any formal lifelong vows taken by priests, deacons, nuns, or other religious. You certainly may separate for good reason without endangering your status as a Catholic, but remarriage while your spouse is still alive would change that. If you have not remarried, you certainly may and should participate in your faith.

Then there's another consideration. Under some circumstances you might qualify for a formal Decree of Nullity (annulment). Regardless of what some people think, this is not at all a "Catholic divorce". A Decree of Nullity is not concerned with the current circumstances of marriage, or how bad things might have become. An annulment is only granted if a thorough and lengthy investigation shows that the marriage did not truly exist to start with. No matter how long you might have been married, or whether there are children, a marriage that originally started with a flaw or any of several valid weaknesses, might be officially declared "null and void", leaving you free to remarry if desired.

Now, if Catholics marry civilly instead of sacramentally (before a judge or an Elvis impersonator), that marriage needs to be blessed in a *convalidation* ceremony. In any event special circumstances apply, and you should consult a qualified priest or deacon for more information, whether the need is for blessing or dissolution.

We want you back fully participating, enjoying the peace of God. Good luck, and have a blessed life!

Come home to me, my precious child, that I may welcome you as my own. Though you have had difficulty and loss in your life, I have never been away from you, and I grieve at your hurt and confusion.

A-14 Question: I was wondering. Can ordinary Catholics administer the Sacraments?

Answer: Yes, that's a good question indeed. That quick answer would normally be "Not on your life; that's reserved for ordained priests and deacons."

However, there indeed are exceptions. The Sacrament of Baptism may be given by a layperson when an unbaptized person is thought to be in danger of death. This is more common than you might think, but the person administering Baptism must use the words given in the bible… "I hereby baptize you in the name of the Father, and of the Son, and of the Holy Spirit, Amen", while pouring moving water over the forehead. If in doubt as to the person having been baptized already, the formula to use is "If thou art not yet baptized, I hereby….." The baptism can be repeated later by an ordained minister if desired and possible, using the second formula. The sacrament of Baptism may be administered only once in life, and causes an irremovable mark on the soul that commits this person to be a child of God.

Any other sacraments? Yes, we are called to hear each other's sins, if there is no church cleric available, and death is near. For practical purposes, this might apply if you happened on a serious accident and a dying person wanted you to be a witness to their sins before the last breath. By all means – hear that confession, but keep it as confidential as would a priest.

The Sacrament of the Sick, at least in extremis, contains an element of reconciliation, and the same applies as above. If necessary due to circumstances, hear that dying confession and give what comfort you can.

Each of the seven major sacraments include an encounter with God that makes internal changes, using external signs such as anointing with oil, pouring of water, hands-on blessings, etc. Under normal circumstances, they remain the province of the ordained.

LORD, I welcome you in each sacrament as we meet and become so much better acquainted. Help me to be wise and forgiving as you are, and to seek you in everything.

A-15 Question: What sacraments does the Catholic Church practice?

Answer: We hold with 7 sacraments that truly involve an interaction with God, and which are visible by the signs, elements and liturgies that surround them. These are, Baptism, Reconciliation, Communion, Confirmation, Marriage, Holy Orders and the Sacrament of the Sick. Of these, all are available to every Catholic except Holy Orders, which involves the ordination of our clergy.

Some other faith expressions hold with fewer sacraments.

I find in your sacraments, O Lord, a reason for being Catholic. That all of life's major events surround me with your love is astonishing, and I rejoice in your eternal embrace. Life can be difficult, and it is with great hope that I look forward to the vision of God's mighty power and beauty at the end of days.

A-17 Question: Are there other ways to be "baptized" into God's family without actually going through the sacramental version? I heard someone say that their parent (deceased) had been saved through a baptism of desire.

Answer: Good question! Yes, being baptized means that you have accepted the precepts of Almighty God, and intend to remain in His graces, to reject Satan, and the other baptismal promises made during the sacrament itself. If, however, you are expecting and looking forward to receiving a traditional baptism, but are called to Heaven before you do so, you can be seen as a true recipient by your "desire" to have had the more usual form.

Also, there is also a Baptism of Blood, in which a person receives martyrdom in defense of his faith. If not previously a recipient of Baptism, there can be no higher statement of being willing to follow God wherever He leads, and that person is truly baptized "by blood".

Remember, though, if the traditional Baptism is used, so must the biblical words, "I hereby baptize you in the name of the Father, and of the Son, and of the Holy Spirit, amen." (While a ritual cleansing of moving water is poured over the forehead.) Baptism may be administered by anyone, believer or not, to a conscious or unconscious recipient, who may or may not have agreed to same if aware – but only when there is an immediate danger of death.

Some faith expressions "baptize" over and over, while we are committed to a belief that it can and need be administered only once. Some also believe that they can "baptize" deceased people, in absentia, even demonstrable un-believers, and even after decades and decades in the grave. Again – impossible, and tragically against the principles of the sacrament itself.

I see the joy in your parents' eyes, oh precious little one. Your godparents, also, and I am struck by the promises made on your behalf. There is so much of life ahead of you, yet your are already pledged to me, and I to you.

A-18 Question: My friend's daughter says she cannot take the Communion host because she's allergic to it. Is there another option?

Answer: So sorry to hear that. This is actually a wide-spread problem. Sufferers from celiac disease cannot tolerate the gluten component of wheat flour. Some are more sensitive than others, but the disease can do great damage to the major organs over time, and cause many interim complications as well. It can even cause fatalities, and is nothing to be taken lightly.

The usual answer is to take communion only from the chalice – Christ's Blood. There is still a completeness – receiving Christ through either species (bread or wine, Body or Blood) is the same. The difference is only a symbolic one, and so we are free to receive both or either. The Church recognizes the consecration only of hosts made from nothing except pure wheat flour and water – the traditional "traveling" flatbread from bible history. They will not permit any deviation. There are "low gluten" hosts available, but that is not the answer if the celiac sensitivity is severe. Hosts made from rice flour or other alternatives cannot be consecrated, and will not – by Church declaration – become the Body of Christ at any time. Some parishes think they are able to experiment with making their own hosts from fancy recipes, but if there are ingredients other than wheat and water, they are way off base. The sacramental wine, by the way, needs only to be pure and natural grape wine of any type – nothing added – and to preferably have a fairly high alcohol content (10 – 15%). However, to make absolutely sure that the wine is pure, the Vatican requires that it be obtained from a very trustworthy source of sacramental vintages.

Regardless of your difficulty, my daughter, I am here already. Know that the desire to be mine, and to take of my Body and Blood have already been such a gift of joy to me! There is nothing that separates us – the Eucharist is already with you – though health issues may have seemed to prevent receiving me as the wafer of Communion .

A-19 Question: The Catholic Church I grew up in never allowed the precious Body and Blood of Christ to be handled by members of the congregation! What gives these days?

Answer: Yes, isn't it wonderful now!? I do understand your question though. I grew up in the 40's and 50's, and you're right – at communion time 3 or 4 priests came out of the sacristy to help the celebrant with service. Women were never allowed past the altar rail during mass. Altar servers held patens under communicants' chins so the host would never be accidentally dropped on the ground. Less than half the congregation would receive at the early masses, and even fewer at the later ones. There was an obligatory fast from anything except water from midnight on. Whew! No wonder people were so reluctant to come to the table of God! Many were so overwhelmed by the sacredness and solemnity of communion that they received no more often than the obligatory once a year.

The Second Vatican Council changed virtually everything. They wanted to make coming to mass an event of and by the people. They wanted the congregation to partake of the entire liturgy, and to start seeing that communion was not scary, but more a gift from God, and that He wanted everybody to see mass as a meal – a sacred feast – a place to come be with His Son – to heal, inspire and nourish without limit or reluctance. The altar rail came down. Priests and altars turned toward us so we could better understand what was happening. The language changed from Latin to the vernacular. The choir was not something we just listened to but celebrated with. We stopped seeing mass happen, and started *being* mass.

The liberals among us were ecstatic. The conservatives said it was disgraceful, and talked of gloomy doom for the Church. But now I see almost everyone partaking of communion, and understanding so much better that each and every person in church makes up the family of God – the living members of the Communion of Saints.

Now, mostly due to the shortage, there are no longer any extra priests hiding in the sacristy until needed to serve communion. The Permanent Diaconate has been reactivated and helps the shortage a bit, but will never be able to keep up with communicants who empty the pews to come and receive. We make an altar of our hands, and stand respectfully for the hosts to be placed there in honor. If we choose to partake of the cup also, we are invited to do so. Those among us who see communion as a sacred and awe-inspiring event are often asked and trained to help distribute alongside the priests and deacons. We were never so richly blessed in previous days, nor had an opportunity to look down and realize just what a privilege it is to hand the Body and Blood to our friends and family.

Many non-ordained ministers of the Eucharist now take communion to the sick, the disabled and the homebound. If priests are unavailable to conduct masses on occasion, trained lay ministers are often authorized to celebrate a simple communion service for the congregation, though only with pre-consecrated hosts. Jesus must be pleased to see communicants coming more than once a year – to join His Family at this – the continuation of the Last Supper. Just – wow!

I am a new minister of the Eucharist, and I tremble as I hold the precious Host, and am weak with joy and fear as I peer deeply into the Cup of Blood that I hand to family and friends. How can this be, that I, a sinner, can receive such an astounding privilege – to hold my

Savior and give to another?

A – 20 QUESTION I'm confused. Did the Sacrament we called Last Rites disappear?

ANSWER: No, it certainly didn't! It was, however, rethought a bit, and then renamed for very good reasons. The Last Rites were permitted to be given to a dying person only once. It involved mostly a strengthening for the journey ahead, as they went into the life beyond the grave. Many, many Catholics lived in dread of seeing a priest come into their hospital room, thinking they might be sicker than they thought. "Come pray with me, Father, but please don't give me the Last Rites!"

The Second Vatican Council, realizing that the actual sacrament was rooted deeply in forgiveness, as well as bringing both spiritual and physical healing to those who were in any danger of death from any reason whatsoever, decided to change things just a bit. They renamed it the "Sacrament of the Sick", available as often as a person was exposed to a potentially deadly experience.

Based on that wonderful passage from the Gospel of John, (Jn20: 22-23), "And when he had said this, he breathed on them and said to them, 'Receive the Holy Spirit, Whose sins you forgive are forgiven them, and whose sins you retain are retained.' ", the church wished to not only bring peace and healing but to also offer true forgiveness for any sins which might burden the person receiving the sacrament. It includes anointing with oils, prayer and – if possible and welcomed –

adds the process of Reconciliation. Those who receive may be conscious or completely unaware, yet the Sacrament remains valid and effective. It is no longer considered a final act in life's journey, nor a frightening experience – merely one which offers much comfort and hope.

Come to me, my Lord, when I am weak and weary – when I am sick unto death. Help me be comforted by the way my life has affected those I treasure, and by the things I have accomplished. Help me to forget those times when I was less than I was meant to be. Guide me home if this is my time, that I may adore my God through eternity.

CHAPTER B - DOCTRINE

B-1 Question: Just when and where did the Catholic Church get its name?

Answer: Well, the first recorded instance that we still have access to of the word "catholic" (*kataholos* in the original Greek) is found in the Letter to the Smymeans written by Ignatius of Antioch in 110 AD. Many other very early writings include the word, simply meant originally to imply "universal". Christ's church started out being called "*The Way*", distinguished by the concept of a single God to be worshiped by the entire world. At the time, most religions honored local "gods", different in each town, province or country. The concept of only one God, a God who created the entire universe, to be universally worshipped throughout the world, was a staggering one. The term "catholic" gradually became the common way to identify this wonderful religion, and eventually the actual, formal name of the Catholic Church.

Blessed Savior, I pledge to remember that your pain, suffering and death were offered up for my spiritual mistakes. I give you in return all that I am and can be, that I may become the person you wish me to be.

B-2 Question: My friend says I shouldn't ever call my priest "Father". Why not?

Answer: Many non-Catholics think we are disobeying Jesus' instruction in Matt 23:9 to "call no man father" when we give that title to our spiritual leaders. Looking around the bible shows how ridiculous this interpretation is. Jesus was telling us to never replace God as the focus of our adoration, since He is indeed our Heavenly Father. The word, when used in an earthly sense to give honor to a parent or a priest, has no intent of dishonoring God. Jesus, Saint Paul and Saint Stephen use the term freely, referring to the responsibility our spiritual leaders have of bringing new life to our souls, and of protecting us from evil influences. How much more "fatherly" could they be?

Priests go through years and years of dedicated study, get degrees in theology and associated majors, and choose to serve all of us without much material reward. Most are not only college graduates, but many have master's and doctoral degrees as well. Shouldn't we be willing to give them our love and support, and show we recognize their special gift to us by calling them Father? If you need biblical references, see Paul's letters 1 Co 4:14, 1 Th 2:11 and Tit 1:4, among many others. I think God understands how we cherish our priests and smiles as we call his special servants by a term of warmth.

Father in heaven, hallowed indeed is your name before all of creation. Continue to support the priesthood of your church in all things, to guide their hearts and teachings, to give them comfort when lonely, to give them energy when they are exhausted, and your love when they are discouraged. Increase their numbers, O Lord, that their labors may be ever more fruitful. In your name, then, we pray.

B-3 Question: A priest once told me that only Catholics can get into Heaven. Is that right?

Answer: Wow! I sure hope you misunderstood that priest! The expression that gives rise to this is "*Extra ecclesia nulils salus.*", which means "*Outside the Church there is no salvation.*", a long-held Christian belief. However, God's Church consists of all persons of good will, faith and morality, regardless of location or religious expression. Yes, as the Church directly started by Jesus, Catholics do feel we have a fullness of doctrine which gives us an edge, but to assume that there are no other people on earth worthy of salvation is a conceit the Church has long grown away from. First of all, I chuckle when people are conceited enough to put words in God's mouth, as if He's not capable or informed enough to make His own decisions. Isn't He all-knowing, all-merciful and all-loving? Who are we to judge anybody's worthiness to be welcomed into God's kingdom? Those who become fully knowledgeable about Christian beliefs and then reject them, however, are undoubtedly on very dangerous ground. Basically, I am a *saint-very-much-in-training*, and try to watch out for my missteps, and to avoid judging what worth God may find in souls other than my own.

Lord, help me to understand that goodness comes not from belonging to one organization, but flows from an inner purity of heart. Let people judge my conviction of faith by the light they may find in my eyes, as much as by the example they may find from the way I live my life.

B-4 Question: I keep hearing about the *Communion of Saints*, but have never understood just what that means. Can you tell me?

Answer: I know that some of our basic beliefs are presumed to be understood by all, especially since we profess belief in the Communion of Saints each Sunday when we recite the Creed. From very early on, the Church has held that there is a unity between all believers who exist in the fullness of God's grace. Thus, all who are now on earth, spiritually pure, are as much members of the Body of Christ as all who have gone on to become God's saints in heaven. Together with the angels, those faithful who have lived in previous times, and the souls in purgatory, these comprise what we call the Communion of Saints. We feel that, being alive in Christ, we have a connection to those souls who have preceded us, as we all give glory to our Creator. Those who have abandoned God on earth and those who are already condemned to hell are not part of the Body of Christ, and therefore not members of the Communion of Saints. I know that my Mom prayed for me every day of my life, and I feel perfectly comfortable asking that she continue to hold me in her thoughts and prayers now that she is with God. Though some other expressions of faith are uncomfortable with the belief that our triumphant and beloved dead have influence with God on our behalf, I have great faith that they remain our greatest supporters and mediators.

All of you worthy souls who live in the glory of God, remember that my journey is still to be completed, and that I am in great need of your example and your remembering me to the Creator whenever possible. Your triumph encourages me when I feel inadequate and sinful, and the light of your purity guides me toward my own goal.

B-5 Question: I've never understood why Catholic priests can't marry. Don't other faiths?

Answer: This is an important question, especially as vocations dwindle at an alarming rate, and the priesthood holds less appeal or seems to receive less respect in this busy, "modern" and self-absorbed world. The Catechism (P1579) states "*All ordained ministers of the Latin Church with the exception of permanent deacons are normally chosen from among men of faith who live a celibate life……*"(Eastern Orthodox branches still allow married priests, but not married bishops).

It has not always been this way. Monks and priests from the infancy of the Church, especially within religious communities, have historically sworn vows of chastity. The practice of celibacy gradually spread to parish priests and became mandatory for parish and religious priests by the mid-1100's. We have a few married priests who come to us from other faiths or branches, and they are welcomed into service after a bit of retraining, but cannot rise above the rank of priest. While we accept the wisdom of our Church authorities, the issue invariably causes debate. Would you be as comfortable going to confession if the priest was a family man? In case of a family conflict, could a married priest choose between a visit to the sick or a child's school recital? Could a priest take a vow of obedience to the Bishop or provincial, knowing that he would be conflicted by family concerns? What about priests who have left active service to become married? We allow divorced or annulled men into seminaries. Can we find a way to bring our married clergy back into the fold? While priests devote their entire lives to serving God's flock, they seldom earn wages comparable to other professions. Are we economically capable of supporting families in the way they would require? I don't know the answers to any of these questions, but they are all valid, widely debated issues.

While celibates may be freer to devote themselves selflessly to parishioners and to their own spirituality, it is sometimes a difficult life. Some seek a release from vows so they can marry. A few become lonely, depressed, or fall into a dependency. Thankfully, though, most thrive in the spiritual environment, the independence, the freedom to live fully in Christ's presence, and the responsibility of providing for their parish families. May God bless their commitment!

Religions similar to Roman Catholicism such as Anglican, Episcopal, etc. generally allow married parish priests, but seldom allow family men to become Bishops, nor do they extend such permission to the missionary or religious orders.

Lord, let us always be mindful of the difficulties our beloved priests suffer in Your service. Let us remember to give them our fullest cooperation, and to keep them in our hearts and prayers at all times.

B-6 Question: My friend tells me I can't earn my way into Heaven. Then how do I get there?

Answer: Sorry, but I'm afraid your friend is right. None of us can *earn* Heaven, but we can certainly throw it away.

Let's say your great uncle Murgatroyd (*yeah, I know, but he never really liked the name "Melvin"*), out of his great love for you, decided to buy you the most wonderful and expensive car in the world. All you really had to do was accept it with thanks. After all, you didn't really work for it – it was a voluntary love gift given out of the sacrifice of many years' earnings. (Stay with me here!) So, instead of doing that, you run off to a life of debauchery and dancing the Hootchie Koo in Kansas City. That car sits there in mint condition, year after year. Your uncle still loves you, and wants you to have it, but it will always be a choice you have to make. Accept the gift, or walk away from it.

The only gift that could have won our salvation was given to us 2000 years ago by Jesus. Our good works can't come close to being enough to "earn" salvation, but they certainly demonstrate our faith, and grow out of a Christian desire to live a useful and loving existence. God tells us to play nice together, and to come see Him when we wear out. However, it will always be our choice to reach out, accept our gift of salvation and join Him in Heaven – or to drift away towards "Kansas City" instead. Heck, the license and insurance are already paid for – just keep "playing nice" – He's waiting!

May you walk in friendship with the Spirit through today's journey, and to continue to be guided toward a oneness with God through all eternity.

<u>B-7 QUESTION</u>: My friends tell me sin doesn't really exist anymore, and that Christ's sacrifice saved us all. Is that true?

<u>ANSWER:</u> Wow, there's been a lot of interest about this lately, and I can assure you that sin, and Satan, exists – always has and always will. God understands our humanity and weakness much better than we do – after all, He made us. We are no longer a church that concentrates on sin, but more on the love we have for each other, and which we can always count on from God. Should we count on His mercy and love? Yes! Should we also be aware that His justice requires obedience, and the penalties for disobedience can be severe and final? Yes – of course! I've always pictured our journey with God a little bit like our experience with early dating. "*Slide over here next to me, honey, so I can put my arm around you.*" Exciting, wasn't it? – full of tender feelings. Eventually, though, the natural progression is that <u>the passenger</u> draws farther away on that front bench seat – not in love, but in space.

So I picture God driving. Sometimes we're close enough for Him to keep His arm around us in love and protection. There are times though, when <u>we</u> choose to slide toward the other side of the "car" by following wrong choices and actions. God sees us slipping away to where we can't feel the warmth of His embrace – but the really neat thing is that the "driver" <u>always</u> stays right there, behind the wheel, ready to put His arm around us whenever we decide to slide back over and be close. Now, if He isn't even in the driver's seat of your particular "car" – you might think about finding a new one!

Jesus, help me to always remember that it was your sacrifice that offered me a chance at eternal salvation. How can I ever forget that your lips formed my name while you suffered, and that your knowledge of my weakness did not in any way cause you to falter on the road to Calvary. I owe you everything, sweetest Jesus, and hope that my journey will eventually bring me proudly into your presence in heaven.

B-8 Question: What does it mean in the Apostles' Creed when it states "*He descended into Hell"*?

Answer: Yes – strange wording, isn't it? That has been a controversial and often misunderstood line throughout Christian history. Many non-Catholic faiths share the Creed with us, but some, including Methodists and Episcopalians have deleted those particular words, due to the confusion they can cause.

The Catholic Church, and most other Christian faith expressions, believes firmly that Jesus, during His stay in the tomb, also descended into the underworld, where there was a place of quiet waiting filled with the slumbering souls of good people, waiting to get into Heaven, which had not yet been opened to humanity. This "hell" was not the place of suffering and torment we usually picture, but an "unseen place of spirits", or "place of separate spirits", as early theologians explained it. St. Aquinas, in the *Summa Theologica*, states: "*He broke down the gate and iron bars of hell, setting at liberty all the righteous who were held fast through original sin.*" Once Christ's sacrifice opened the gates of Heaven, these good souls could finally "come home*"*. (see also: St. Paul's statement in Col 2:15 and *The*

Catechism of the Catholic Church, #631 through 637)

We now usually say "*He descended to the dead*", as perhaps a more easily understood way of expressing this belief. When the Apostles' Creed was updated by the Council of Nicaea in 325 AD, the line was left out, though it remained in many other versions of the Creed (Athanasian, Acquelian, Received and Gallican).

Lord, I know that though I live, sometimes I feel spiritually dead. With a heavy heart, I come to you, asking again for your forgiveness and understanding. How is it that you smile eagerly – that your angels sing to me so sweetly – that your embrace enfolds me before I can even ask? Your compassion and love are endless, and with your help I will find salvation!

B-9 Comment: (recently heard) I hate God! I've had nothing but trouble in my life. How could He do this to me!

Answer: Gosh, I wish I had pages and pages to answer this one! God created you, personally – and loves you like an only child. However, living in comfort and ease has never been guaranteed to anyone. Just ask the hundreds of billions of dead humans – "*Was your life easy?*" The answer would always be, "*Absolutely not, but there were joys and triumphs, too*!" If there were no effort in life – no obstacles to overcome, there would never be growth of character. Couch potatoes get soft and fat. Athletes become strong through pain and effort, and can accomplish great things. Nobody, NOBODY, escapes tragedy, loss, struggle and trial. Only those who overcome the challenges of life can appreciate the joy, beauty and triumph that surround us always. Life is hard! Yes – but don't blame God! Blame humanity! Human weakness, greed and self-interest are everywhere. Violence, war – struggle for power, intolerance, sin and hate.

Can we see beyond that to a family's love, to the beauty of sunsets, rolling surf, a baby's first step? Every tear is offset by eventual laughter, by joy. Don't blame God for your pain and struggle; just thank Him every minute for His love and support, and for offering you an eternal reward for not giving up or giving in. Does He answer your prayers? – of course! As the saying goes, though, in His wisdom the answers range from "*yes*", to "*no*", to "*maybe*", and to "*not just yet*". May we all find the loving humility to accept the answer, whatever it may be.

May God grant us the strength to always see Him as the source of all that is good!

B-10 Question: My minister says that belief in Purgatory is nonsense – that Catholics "invented" it. What about it?

Answer: Again – a big subject, but as starting point, our Catholic Catechism defines Purgatory as a "*purification, so as to achieve the holiness necessary to enter the joy of heaven, for those who die in God's grace and friendship, but (are) still imperfectly purified.*" (CCC 1030) No, the belief that a purification process is absolutely necessary somewhere between the tortures of the truly damned, and those already pure and complete in God's Kingdom has been proclaimed from the earliest days of the Apostles.

True, the word "Purgatory" came later, as did the words "Trinity" and "Incarnation", but the Church has always taught the essence behind all three terms, words which are man-made, but do sufficiently describe the concepts. Jesus himself refers to one who "*will not be forgiven, either in this age or in the age to come"* (Mt 12:32) suggesting that *some* sinners can and will be forgiven *after death*. Christians and Jews alike have always believed in a "*dusting off and polishing up*" period to take care of whatever minor sins we may have taken to the grave, but which are not sufficiently serious to prevent our eventual entry into the wonders of the Kingdom! Many other scriptural references pronounce the existence of a penitential state, and we truly believe "*nothing unclean shall enter Heaven.*" *(See you later – I've got a bunch of "polishing" to do!)*

B-11 Question: I've heard that the Catholic Church is distinguished by four marks. What does that mean, exactly.

Answer: During the Apostles Creed, we say that we truly, deeply believe that the church is "one, holy, catholic and apostolic." These are the four marks, and they do distinguish the uniqueness of our faith.

We are one, united with our brethren throughout the world and through the Communion of Saints in our beliefs, our prayers and our liturgies. Anywhere in the world you find Catholics, you will find the exact same doctrines, practices and mass.

The church is holy, having been formed by Christ, who is holiness itself.

The church is catholic (please note the small "c") meaning it is intended to honor only one God, creator of everything, and to be a church for the entire world – a universal church. The original term for this faith was *The Way*, but the Greeks began to call it *Ecclesia Catolica*, or "universal church", and the term stuck, becoming finally the name we use today to signify those faith expressions which acknowledge the authority of the Pope of Rome. There are 23 of those, including Roman Catholicism (the western church), and 22 Eastern Catholic Churches.

The church is apostolic , not only because the 12 Apostles served as founders of the faith, but it is much more than that. Yes, the core group that we are familiar with were called apostles, but there were others called that as well. The church continues to be based on apostolic leadership, and each member asked to continue answering a call of spreading the Gospel, the *Good News.* There is a 2000 year continuation of passing along the authority granted by Jesus to be missionaries in our daily lives. Each bishop and priest has received that authority by a hands-on blessing from those who went before them, all the way back to the Great Commissioning of Saint Peter by Jesus. We are each called to a spiritual kingship in our lives, according to the order of Melchizedek, King of Salem, type of Jesus the Messiah, though our priesthood is more delineated than that allowed to our ordained ministers, whether bishops, priests or deacons.

I also, Lord, am marked. My baptism has kept me closer to you than I could ever have imagined, and my soul bears the brand of your love. Hold and comfort me, my Savior, as I struggle with life and all it entails. When I come before you, that brand will set me in a special part of your heart, where I can forever offer you praise and glory.

B-12 Question: Does the local ordinary (diocesan bishops or parish pastors, the "ordinary" source of authority within their jurisdiction) have the authority to grant exemptions from some laws of the church?

Answer: Yes, they do have some latitude to exercise their judgment in special circumstances. The code of canon law, which is the basic guide to all legality within the church, for instance, permits them to bless (convalidate) some previously non-recognized marriages, without taking the matter before the Tribunal, the court of canon law.. Similarly, some annulments may be expedited under pastoral compassion, etc. However, such decisions are usually done "*in camera*" which means *in darkness*. The action taken must not cause scandal or visible dissension from the norm, and so these situations call for discretion and quiet proceedings. Can. 1130

The church which you have established, Lord, sees your children with compassion, and nourishes them with love.

B-13 Question: What punishments can the Church impose on disobedient Catholics?

Answer: This is probably one of those subjects whose rarity will almost never impact our own daily lives. However, just to answer, people who present an unabashed and public disavowal of their faith, or cause public scandal by participating in the sacraments after taking a stand against our basic principals can be excommunicated. Recently a major political figure was asked to discontinue taking the Eucharist, since she continually encouraged women to receive abortions. Her not being allowed to be "in communion" with the rest of the faithful is a drastic, seldom-taken step. Priests who abandon their vow of chastity, marry, and continue to practice their priesthood, can undergo excommunication. This punishment can sometimes be lifted by repentance, public renouncement of previous errors, and appeals to the Vatican.

Other steps within the concept of excommunication can be taken such as *shunning* in which church authority requires that the faithful not associate with, talk to or support someone who is publically heretical. This punishment can be extremely difficult to endure. It is more often used in some other faith expressions, such as the Latter Day Saints, using *shunning* to punish and control those who disagree with current doctrine or practices.

For priests who seek to be relieved from the burden of their vows of chastity and obedience, they may apply to the Vatican for *laicization*. This, when and if granted, returns them to being members of the lay people. While not really a punishment, it can be fairly traumatic for an ordained priest to lose his right to consecrate the Eucharist and to cease being a functioning shepherd for his flock.

Your religion, my Lord, is not one of punishment and reprisal, but one of welcoming, forgiveness and understanding. If, for the good of the whole, sometimes one of your flock must be separated from it, keep them in your counsel and comfort them with your embrace. Let your love return them to us healed and whole.

B-14 Question: Is there anything special about the materials used to make the sacred hosts and the precious wine?

Answer: The host must contain nothing but pure wheat flour and water. Usually this wheat itself is taken from a chemical-free portion of the farmland. Some parishes have tried to make their own using strange recipes that include salt, sugar, honey and other ingredients in addition, but that is contrary to church law.

Hosts are generally made by religious communities, who use the funds to support themselves and their works. Sacramental wines, however, are easily sourced from most reputable wine merchants, and can even be home produced, but it must absolutely remain untouched by any adulterating ingredients.

Sacramental wine must be made only from grapes, unadulterated with other juices, added sugar; not fortified with added alcohol or anything else. It may be whatever type is natural - sweet, tart, white, red, etc., but must not have additional ingredients. It is also required to have an innate high alcohol content, (between 10 and 15% preferably) by nature, to give the added element of self-purification as people take from the communion cup. I read somewhere of studies to determine whether or not disease has ever transferred between communicants who take from the chalice, and was not surprised to see that there has never been a record of that happening. Christ's Blood is sacred and safe!

A study first published in 1943 in the Journal of Infectious Diseases, and later reprinted and restudied many times reports that virtually no bacteria can be found on the rim of chalices which have been wiped by a purificator. (the linen cloth used by the minister of Communion). Studies done specifically about that concern have been done at the University of Chicago, and in 1997 a publication of the Felician College in New Jersey showed studies done comparing health issues of non-communicants and communicants, and found no statistical difference whatsoever.

Still – in flu season, be practical! Remember too, the Body of Christ, which is each of us gathered as God's family, is a form of Holy Eucharist also, as we celebrate being in the special presence of God's favored Son.

B-15 Question: I've heard the term "being scrupulous" as a bad thing. What exactly is that?

Answer: Well, we all hope that our actions satisfy God's directive to live in His grace. Sometimes we start examining every facet of living to see if we might be giving Him offense, to the point that our faith life and our joy of life is crippled by in an unhealthy fixation with "being perfect". A scrupulous person lives in doubt, and in an agony of feeling deeply and irredeemably sinful. It is a mental, emotional and spiritual fault, which denies the wonder of Almighty God, and His relationship with us. All of us recognize that we are not yet perfect; that each of us is still a sinner, and that God loves and understands our nature, granting forgiveness anytime we ask for it. Scrupulosity, which denies even the possibility of such love and understanding is sinful, demonstrates spiritual despair, and threatens our faith lives.

Often, the feeling of inadequacy and indecision, and a constant introspection that we consider scrupulosity is a symptom of deeper mental disturbances (such as OCD) that needs treatment, rather than condemnation.

Lord, though I may be deeply loved by you, I know there are times when my lack of spirituality may disappoint you. Be patient, my love, and I will return.

<u>B-16 Question:</u> Why do we bow to the book that the priest carries to the microphone during mass.

<u>Answer:</u> This is the Book of Gospels, which contains the written Word of God, but also quotes the very words of Jesus as recorded by the Four Evangelists, Matthew, Mark, Luke and John.

As a symbol of our deep respect for this sacred scripture, we stand and/or bow as it passes by. We continue standing as the priest reads from the Gospel of the day. As he says, "This is the Gospel according to…", we also sign ourselves with the cross on the forehead, lips and breast. This signifies, and should always be brought to mind, that we hope these words will *come to rest deeply in our <u>minds</u> so that we may learn from them*; that *they will rest on our <u>lips</u>,* that we may spread them through our apostleship; and that *they will come to rest in our <u>hearts</u>*, that we may love and treasure them forever.

Please be assured, though, that if your physical condition is such that you cannot or should not participate in the Catholic sit, stand and kneel sequences, feel perfectly free to sit in the pew throughout the mass.

Here I am at mass again, my Jesus. Help me to pay attention to your wondrous presence, to hear your words with understanding and patience, and to be aware of always of the reality of receiving the very Body and Blood during communion.

B-17 Question: Why is the Church permitted to make rules for us that exceed those brought to us by Jesus?

Answer: This is a very common question. Some rules have been added through the centuries to remind Catholics of the basic truths and doctrines of the Church. Thus, we are required to attend mass on Sundays since our clergy is well aware that many times we might be tempted by a good soccer or baseball game to distract us; that there are times when we'd be tempted to just sleep in, go to a picnic or get involved in worldly events instead of keeping some time for worshiping our God. Small sacrifices such as the very limited fasting and abstaining we currently practice remind us of Christ's sacrifice on the cross for our sins. Many other things are used to encourage us in faith, and none of these reflect the false and burdensome rules that Jesus used to condemn, as imposed by the Pharisees.

The Church maintains that it is perfectly in the right to make guidelines of faith for us to participate in – based on what is called the Great Commissioning. (see Mt 28:18-20) "Then Jesus approached and said to them, 'All power in heaven and on earth has been given to me. / Go, therefore, and make disciples of all nations, baptizing them in the name of the Father, and of the Son, and of the Holy Spirit, / teaching them to observe all that I have commanded you. And behold, I am with you always, until the end of the age'."

These words, and others in different gospels, told the new church leaders to forgive sins as they saw fit, that their decisions in such forgiveness would be honored in heaven, etc. They felt rightly that this gave them authority to teach and lead in such a way that the new faith would be held preciously; that the leaders should do whatever was needed to bring the concept of one God, one creation, one world, one religion to fruition. If church man-made rules helped that to happen, it was a righteous endeavor. Know, though, that rules imposed by God comprise doctrine which cannot be changed, but man-made ones can be altered when necessary. Without such reinforcement of faith, we could easily drift away from Christ's beautiful church.

In your infinite knowledge and wisdom, my God, you protect and keep your church safe and secure. Let your leaders act with similar wisdom and compassion as they seek to spread your Gospel.

B-18 Question: Is it still Catholic doctrine that all persons who have passed away may only be buried, never cremated?

Answer: No, not necessarily. That was meant to demonstrate our belief there would eventually be a resurrection of the body at the end of time. Destroying whatever integrity the body happened to maintain might have shown the world that we did not believe in a final bodily resurrection. Keeping the remains as intact as possible demonstrates our faith in that resurrection. Of course, God can and will accomplish that without any difficulty, regardless of what has happened to the body. After all, wars, natural disasters, shipwrecks, disease and the like have always made a complete recovery of body parts or remains impossible or impractical.

Now we are simply asked to maintain a reverence for the remains, demonstrating our respect for the dead, for all they have accomplished in life, and who we now are certain have gone on to a spiritual reward. Thus, burial in ground or mausoleums would still be a church preference, but cremation is permitted, though with conditions. The ashes must remain in a place of respect and reverence. Spreading those ashes over the ground or the sea, or keeping them on a dusty fireplace mantle does not fit the church's perception of keeping the remains intact and honored.

Offer your faithful consolation when their loved ones pass to your reward. We don't know how to live without them in our midst, or how to run our lives without their smiling friendship to guide us. See us bleed with our grief. See us stumble in our confusion. See us needing your comfort!

B-19 Question: Is the concept of Limbo as a place for dead unbaptized innocents still a church belief?

Answer: No, its not. We try not to put words in God's mouth, nor pretend to understand the depth of His compassion and mercy. When St. Augustine was asked that question, he simply scratched his head and replied that he had no idea – their fate was in limbo as far as he was concerned. He meant that their fate was unknown, and simply up to God's grace to determine. However the word somehow evolved into unofficial Catholic doctrine, but has lately and rightly been purged.

Forgive us our confusion, O Lord, and keep us on the path toward your goodness.

B-20 Question: Does the term "*informed conscience*" mean we can choose which rules or commandments we want to follow?

Answer: No, it sure doesn't. St. Catherine of Siena explained it well. "Your conscience is like a guard dog that barks and alerts you to evil, sin, temptation, etc. But, you have to feed the dog. If you don't feed him, he becomes weaker and weaker until he no longer barks anymore. We have to feed our conscience with the word of God as proclaimed and taught by Holy Church."

And so an "*informed conscience*" is simply that – a healthy safeguard against making imprudent decisions about faith, God's rule for our lives and understanding Church requirements as well. The Second Vatican Council recognized, however, that we are all people of intellect and free will, and should be able to examine those regulations that impact our lives, then gauge them in the light of a fully, healthily mature conscience. If that is done – if your conscience is alive and well – if you pray over your decision – if you accept that a mistake in judgment may be seriously sinful – then you may make a choice about whether or not to obey a law. Realize though, that this sets you outside the framework of faith embraced by the Church, and makes you responsible for any negative spiritual results for your independence. Bottom line, flying solo is very dangerous, and not something I would recommend. Always consult with a priest when conflicts arise.

Give me the gift of a renewed and dependable conscience, O God, that I may better understand how I may approach you in pride at the end of my days.

B-21 Question: Are we still as Catholics required to attend mass on Sunday?

Answer: Well, that sounds like going to mass is something terrible. I personally wouldn't want you to have to do something that you hate. However, the mass I know is lively, rich in substance and meaning. The fellowship with other parishioners is warm and welcoming, the reception of the Eucharist is faith-building – what's so bad?

So yes, the official answer would still be that we are required to attend mass on Sundays, whether it be a vigil service on Saturday evening, or one during the day on Sunday. That presupposes that you are healthy, have a way to get to church, are not attending to something else that is quite serious, etc. God said "*Keep the Sabbath holy*". If you are traveling more than 50 miles from home, have other issues that make it extremely difficult or unwise to get to church, you are obviously excused, but still – try to find some holiness in the day nonetheless. The Church in its wisdom and authority knows that we are all lazy enough to fall away from mass attendance unless we are required to be there.

When my family travels, we find it exciting and interesting to find a local mass wherever we happen to be, and regardless of the language being used. We've done that in many countries, and in many, many small towns in the States.

Now, if your conflict arises from something frivolous and self-centered – (got free tickets to the Dodgers?) – I'd recommend you find a way to include God, preferably at mass, in your day. Ask a priest to excuse you, at least.

B-22 Question: Why don't we allow women priests in the Catholic Church?

Answer: Ah, well, ahem, uh…that's certainly a valid question, (can you tell this is also one which raises strong reactions?)

We all look at the shortage of priests, at the impossibly heavy burden of service they deal with every day of their lives, and the difficulty of trying to be the answer to everybody's problems – how do they do it? They are dedicated people, yet still just guys trying to do what they can to promote God's message. Their lives are as messy and troubled as our own, but we allow them very little understanding sometimes. Make this your "take a priest out to lunch or dinner" month, and consider them a friend.

Most other faith expressions allow women to become priests, deacons, elders, pastors, ministers, etc. The Catholic Church has reviewed this over and over through the centuries. They continually say the original 12 were all men, ignoring much of history – women disciples, women supporting the Christian movement with their riches, women martyrs, women saints, women of spiritual power. There are other reasons, of course, but perhaps not insurmountable ones.

Know that Pope John Paul II made a very definitive statement on May 22, 1994. *"Wherefore in order that all doubt may be removed regarding a matter of great importance, a matter which pertains to the church's divine constitution itself, in virtue of my ministry of confirming the Brethren, I declare that the Church has no authority whatsoever to confer priestly ordination on women, and that this judgment is to be definitively held by all the Church's faithful.* " A statement this absolute seems to prevent much wiggle room about Church belief.

The latest word from the Vatican – The Sacred Congregation for the Doctrine of Faith, the successor to the department that led the Inquisition during the middle ages – also came out with a decisive ruling on the subject in 2008 - "Only a baptized man validly receives sacred ordination." Thus it remains vividly official doctrine, which we are obligated to observe.

There are many, many dissenting groups within and without the Catholic faith, some of which have been excommunicated as a result of their views. My personal view: I think it may be an inevitable necessity, and personally would be acceptable to me. While the Church claims it is a divine law that only men can ascend to ordination, and therefore an unchangeable doctrine of faith, there are those who claim it is merely a man-made desire to keep the priesthood a male dominion. I will, however, support the Vatican solidly as their wise counsel dictates, hoping that something will eventually bring us the gift of more persons eligible and desirous of becoming priests, God's holy people.

Help me to see the wisdom of those whom you have called to be your bishops, O Lord, to understand their deliberations and decisions, and to support them in their difficult works.

B-23 Question: Do you believe in the existence of angels?

Answer: Yes, I certainly do! If the bible reflects the truths of God, there are endless references that reflect the reality of angels. Do I understand exactly what they are, what they look like, what their roles are in my life, how they relate to God – no. The concept of angelic beings actually originated with the Egyptians, then came through Judaism, and fully into Christian beliefs. Many of the Church fathers have expounded on them, and there are references in, for instance, Psalms 8:4-5, Psalms 148:2-5, Colossians 1:16, , and many other biblical passages. Jesus spoke of them, and He should know!

The First Vatican Council (325) and the Fourth Lateran Council (1215) wrote scholarly reviews on God's messengers, etc., and St. Thomas Aquinas includes angelology (the study of angels) in several writings, including *Summa Theologica.*

The pervading thought is that angels are created beings, pure spirits, called into existence for service to God before humans were conceived. They perform many different functions, including adoration of God's majesty, serving as His messengers to humanity, helping guide and protect each of us individually, and as warriors against Satan. Satan himself and his demons are said to be angels who rebelled against God and were cast away from the Beatific

Vision, into Hades. Their demonic influence in our lives is to tempt us away from God, while the angelic host does the opposite.

We have apparent names only for a few: Gabriel, Ariel, Michael, Raphael, (and, of course, Lucifer).

The New Testament lists angels in Lk 1:11, Lk 1:26, Lk 2:10, Mt4:11, Lk 22:43, Mt 28:5, Mt 24:36 and Heb12:2.

Humans are able to grasp God's domain only through the filter of our limited existence. We are people confined to a progression of "time", and we are never going to be able to "create". We can make, we can alter, we can use and we can discover, but to actually create something from nothing – never. God can. God exists outside any constraints of "time", and we cannot conceive of that concept. We will never, in this life, be able to picture the divine, the unlimited, the all-powerful. A belief in angels, simple. Belief in the other things we cannot understand or perceive with our senses – can only come through faith.

Oh you of the angelic host, who watch and protect us in our faltering faith lives, continue to counsel us, and invoke the Almighty to bless us endlessly as we struggle with our weaknesses.

<u>B-24 Question:</u> Ok, well then, that said – just what is Faith?

Answer: Faith is the ability and determination to believe those things which exist, but which we cannot find with our senses – touch, sight, taste, hearing. Instead, we must rely on other information – that which God the Father, Jesus and the Holy Spirit have revealed, which history has recorded and brought forward, and what the body of Church authority has made doctrine.

In our everyday lives, we can take with faith that the cars coming at us on the highway at 70 mph will not cross into our right of way. We can trust that our specialized scientists can get hardware into orbit without our being able to fathom how they do it. We have faith in each other, especially our partners in life. For us to extend faith into a belief that there exists a supreme being is not really difficult. We have faith that evil exists, perhaps only as an absence of God's goodness, and that there is an afterlife awaiting us if we choose to accept the conditions for it's achievement. What can be a challenge is to nourish and enrich that faith over time, and to carry it throughout our lives, even when hardship wants us to falter.

My faith follows a very difficult path, my God. Help me as I struggle!

B-25 Question: How can we say that we have a God who is also three independent persons?

Answer: An everlasting mystery – a mysterious conundrum, isn't it? But, if we have faith in what God the Father has revealed to us, we have been told that he and the Son are one, that they are each fully participators in creation, that neither of them has a beginning nor an end, and that their perfect love for each other can be called the Holy Spirit. In Genesis, the bible says God speaks of himself in the plural. In Jesus we have declarations of his relationship with the Father. He also says that he will send a Paraclete (intercessor) after He has left the world to instruct, protect and guide us.

No, we don't understand how these things can be, but we definitely recognize them as truths, believing them in faith. Saint Patrick made an unforgettable comparison between the Irish Shamrock, which had 3 leaflets on one stem, and the Trinitarian Godhead. If it makes it easier, simply consider them to be the various personalities of God, or the 3 members of one very close family. Regardless, we see the Father in just that light, the Son as the savior of mankind through His sacrifice, and the Holy Spirit to be that aspect of God which works throughout the human race.

"*Glory be to the Father, and to the Son, and to Holy Spirit, as it was in the beginning, is now, and ever shall be, world without end. Amen*"

B-26 Question: Is everything the Pope states considered infallible?

Answer: Everything the Pope states officially is wonderful guidance for our lives, and reflects his view as Vicar of Christ. The infallibility issue comes when he endorses some particular belief as doctrine that must be believed by all Catholics, and he at that time must be speaking *ex cathedra*, "from the throne of Peter". In other words, he is invoking his authority to do so as the head of God's church on Earth – the leader of the Catholic faith. There have only been two instances wherein a pope has officially done so:

Pope Pius IX, on December 8th, 1854 declared infallibly that the Blessed Virgin had been conceived in her mother's womb without sin – The Immaculate Conception. That feast day takes place on December 8th each year.

Pope Pius XII, on November 1, 1950 declared infallibly that the Blessed Virgin had been assumed body and soul into heaven upon her death. This feast of the Assumption of the Blessed Virgin Mary is recognized on August 15th each year.

In order to be an infallible utterance by a pope, he must state that he is putting his entire authority behind the issue. It must also be a doctrine that has always had the full belief of the Catholic faith behind it through the ages, and thus has an informal but full approval of Catholic believers already, and it must pertain to faith and morals. It is usually done only to prevent mistaken beliefs or misdirected teachings that contravene the popular perception of certain issues, and seem to be causing concern among God's followers.

And so, are other statements from the Pope to be considered infallible? No, usually not, though they are to be taken as official direction and may illustrate or validate official doctrine. That does not in any way diminish their importance, nor lessen the requirement that we be guided by his words. However, the mandatory "belief" of an infallible document can be lacking to some degree. Some encyclicals and other publications of pontiffs through the centuries may actually have an aspect of infallibility, lacking only the formal papal invocation of "*ex cathedra*".

Though I know the Pontiff seldom invokes his right to speak from the Throne of Peter, my God, help me to find wisdom and guidance in everything which he teaches.

B-27 Question: I have non-Catholic friends, good people, who tell me we are all forgiven our sins through the crucifixion and death of Jesus, and thus have salvation promised regardless of our actions. Does that sound right?

Answer: Sorry, that is a common belief among some Christian faiths, but I'm afraid it is more wishful thinking than otherwise.

If nothing else, let's look at the letters of Paul: 1Cor10-12 "Let anyone who thinks he is standing upright watch out lest he fall."

2Cor5:10 "The lives of all of us are to be revealed before the tribunal of Christ so that each one of us may receive his recompense, good or bad, according to his life in the body."

1Cor9:26-27 "...What I do is discipline my own body and master it, for fear that after having preached to others I myself should be rejected."

Rom 11:22 "Consider the kindness and the severity of God; severity toward those who fell, kindness toward you, provided you remain in his kindness; if you do not, you too will be cut off."

These all state that we must each remain worthy of salvation – if we do not – if we return to or remain in our sin – we will not see salvation, even if we expect to do so.

Help me to approach your throne without trepidation or fear, my God, knowing that I have kept the faith, and passed through the door of death without serious sin on my soul.

B-28 Question: Is Satan real? I notice that the RCIA people are going through Scrutinies on the 3rd, 4th, and 5th Sundays of Lent, and I hear these include exorcisms, which sounds scary.

Answer: Well.... of course!!! Christian tradition states that God created angels, one of whom rebelled out of pride, was expelled from Heaven by St. Michael the Archangel, and thrown down with many, many followers. Though there is no exact Bible passage describing that battle, the existence of personified evil is spoken of throughout scripture. *Devils and demons – oh my!* However, Lucifer, (translated as *Light of the Morning Star*), would have been truly intelligent and beautiful to behold. His influence over us is ever present and often very subtle. Never forget, Satan and his minions are as close to you as your next breath, just waiting for the slightest misstep. We are under attack at all times, as evil forces try to lead us toward damnation. Don't look for ugliness or for beings in red tights holding pitchforks, but for beings of great influence trying to sway us from God's teachings and grace. Evil and sin exists, and these are not Halloween jokes. You are always free to make the moral and ethical choices to either achieve the triumph of Heaven or to lose the eternal vision of God, an existence we call Hell. Weigh your life decisions very carefully! Exorcisms? – yes, asking that Satan remove himself from influencing your life! This is an important prelude to becoming a newly baptized and confirmed child of God through the RCIA process.

Oh Lord, give me the strength of faith, the courage I lack and the wisdom I need to know your presence in my life. Help me hold fast to my baptismal promise to reject the influence of Satan and to always seek to be worthy of the salvation promised to all who live daily in the security and warmth of your grace.

B-29 QUESTION I hear terms around the church that I don't understand, like tradition and something like "majesty"? What do these have to do with Catholicism?

ANSWER: Yes, we throw words around as if everybody knew what we're talking about, don't we?

These, however, are really very important in understanding anything about holy scripture, and the right of the Church to make rules, which can be a point of contention sometimes.

Tradition is that body of history that started out as word-of-mouth experiences that were passed down intact from generation to generation until they were finally recorded as written history – scripture, starting probably about 1800 years before Jesus. Still, historical events, and religious wonders were not always submitted as "scripture" and written down on scrolls. There was a living, breathing body of truth and experience besides, that continually evolved and recorded events, and that "tradition" was both/either word-of-mouth, or writings in addition to what was considered Holy Scripture. Tradition that became written down was responsible for the 46 (or 39) books from which the Jewish nation read in Temple or synagogue, but it also existed outside of, and in support of those books.

When the New, Christian Testament began with the birth of the Man/God, Jesus the Messiah who had been foretold for centuries, those who were closest to him during His public ministry talked about their experiences for many years. Word-of-mouth tradition! They taught from their knowledge, and passed it along to other generations. Finally, as much at 60 years after Jesus died, these experiences had been put down in writing. Scriptural tradition! As many as 33 "gospels" have been uncovered over the years, though only those which best served the purpose of informing the followers of Christ were finally accepted as genuinely inspired by God, and put into the "canon" of scripture. (Canon simply means that group which the Church deems to be true and sufficient) There is so much wonderful resource material in addition to those written of in the 27 books of the New Testament! Those resources offer an amazing wealth of religious inspiration, and that body of knowledge is being continually being built up still today. They include the scholarship of the Doctors of the Church, of theologians and historians, of the 21 general Councils of the Church, of the leadership and continuity of bishops and pontiffs who have guided us to today. Think of the uncounted millions of volumes of wisdom held within the Vatican Library alone! Are these not worth their weight in gold? The Dead Sea Scrolls, discovered only in the 1940's, have been a source of wonders, and new resources are continually surfacing or evolving. .

Truth: All of sacred Scripture is wonderful. Also truth! - not all things wonderful are contained within those 73 books – Sacred Tradition exists in addition to and in support of sacred Scripture.

That other word you were searching for was probably ***Magisterium***, which is a Latin word that means "authority to teach". Take a look at Acts 2:8, John 21:31, Mark 16:14-16 and Mt 28:19-20. In these Jesus cumulatively says: "All power in heaven and on earth has been given to me. Go therefore and make disciples (followers, students) of all nations, baptizing them in the name of the Father, and of the Son, and of the Holy Spirit, **teaching** them to observe all that I have commanded you. And behold, I am with you always, until the end of the age." Also we have the command from Jesus to Peter: "Peter, thou art 'Rock', and I will build my church upon you, and give you the keys to the Kingdom of Heaven. And behold, whatever you loose (forgive) on earth will be forgiven in Heaven, and whatever you hold (don't forgive) on earth will be held in Heaven."

And so, during what we consider the "Great Commissioning", the Church has been mandated to "forgive or not forgive", and to "teach and baptize the entire world". This demand – this authority from Jesus Himself – the Church takes very seriously, and so teaches in such ways that seem necessary to preserve the sacred body of knowledge and the new church established by Christ. The structure of Catholic faith recognizes a duty and right to hear the sins of followers, and to forgive or not, in Christ's name. Scripture is a living example of God's Word, as is Sacred Tradition, and, actually, as are you and I as we live lives which influence the thoughts and actions of others.

This sacred duty to follow Christ's instructions is what has kept the Catholic Church intact and true to its beginnings through the last 20 centuries, and will continue to do so as long as life exists on earth.

Thank you, my God, for in your great wisdom, you have left our spiritual care in such good hands.

B-30 Question: I hear the word (cannon?) or canon sometimes in reference to the bible. What does that mean, exactly?

Answer: Well, I think the word you heard is probably "canon". In ancient times, a ruled wooden or metal rod was used to verify the quantity of grain in a container. This rod was called a *canon*, and the term came to mean something true and certifiable.

When a list of potential writings were studied by the bishops present at the Councils of Nicaea and Constantinople, a list of books which they thought to be certifiably inspired by God was proposed and accepted. This became the unofficial "canon" of Holy Scripture, which included 46 books from the Jewish Testament, and 27 books from the New Testament. This was finally endorsed as the official list at the Council of Trent, about 1550. All modern bibles endorsed for Roman Catholic use now contain the same 73 volumes, while most non-Catholic faith expressions use 7 less volumes in the Old Testament.

So, when you hear that the Church "canonized" someone as a saint, know that they are putting their reputation behind that announcement, certifying their decision as accurate and verifiable.

Lord, we acknowledge the inspired works of scripture left to us by the founders of the Church, and thank you for providing such a great source of wisdom, courage, hope and faith. Thank you so much!

CHAPTER C - CATHOLIC PRACTICES

C-1 Question: I study and pray at home constantly, but seldom feel really close to God. What's wrong?

Answer: We all have dry spells in our spirituality, but the cycle will always bring us back to our usual certainty of faith. Home bible study, etc., is never a bad thing, but God can be more visibly present in other settings. Remember the familiar words of the mass, when the priest states "*The Lord is with you!*", and we respond, "*and also with you*!" The first time we hear this is as thc assembly gathers and becomes, literally, the Body of Christ. God is present and close – for "*whenever two or three are gathered in my name, there am I in the midst of them." Mt 18:20* The second time we hear that is just before the Gospel, when we are reminded that God is always found present in his holy Word – the scriptures. The third time the statement is made is just as the parish gifts of bread and wine become the Body and Blood of salvation. Wow! – is God vividly in our midst at that point!

Solitary prayer, bible study and even things like nature appreciation are all vital to our spiritual growth, but always seek out the family of God through the parish assembly, hopefully at more times than just Sunday mass, for a true experience of God's closeness.

Give me, my God, the gift of determination, that I may know your Word through the sacred scripture, so to teach and lead others, and to bring your guidance into the whole of my own life.

C-2 Question: Lent will be starting pretty soon. I never understand why I'm supposed to be sorrowful when Easter is coming.

Answer: Lent is supposed to be a time when we prepare, not only for the glory of Easter, but also for the passion and death of Jesus, who died that our sins might find forgiveness. So our sorrow urges us to examine ourselves for sins and faults that might be keeping us away from His side, and to remove those stains through penance and absolution. Through our very mild days of Lenten fast and/or abstinence, we try to remind ourselves of the deep sacrifices Jesus made for us, and ask how we can become more worthy of His love. Then, cleansed, we can truly rejoice as our Lord rises from death at Easter!

Maybe this Easter, I will have found your peace and your purpose for my life through my experiences of Lent, of your passion and death, and in the exultation of your rising from death itself.

C-3 Question: I get blessed with ashes each Lent, but don't really understand the significance. So – what's it about?

Answer: Every Ash Wednesday marks the beginning of Lent, an

annual 6-week period of penance and reflection leading up to Holy Week, where Christ's passion and death brings us the possibility of salvation.

The ancient practice of wearing ashes (which used to involve wearing sackcloth and LOTS of ashes to humble ourselves) wants us to recall that our bodies were created as temporary residences, eventually to be discarded, and that our eternal souls need to be our real concern. Forget mortal vanity! The older instruction given by the priest when applying the cross of ashes "*Remember man – thou art dust, and to dust thou shalt return!*" reminded us to keep priorities straight. A newer message, now in more common use, asks us to *"Repent from sin and be faithful to the Gospel."* (and there are other blessings in use also.) This blessing with ashes is a symbolic event, not a sacrament, and can be received by anybody of faith.

On Palm Sunday, one week before the cruel death of Jesus on the Cross, the crowds welcomed him into Jerusalem with great joy, spreading palm branches before Him. Several days later the same crowds shouted, "Crucify Him!". We also receive palm fronds each year, to remind us how fickle human emotions can be, and to emphasize that it was specifically for my sins, and yours, that Christ died. The fronds left over from last Palm Sunday are ceremonially burned each year, to become the ashes used on Ash Wednesday. *(Feel free to bring your old "palms" to the parish center for recycling!)*

Be proud to receive and wear that small sign each Lenten season symbolizing you are a person of respect and faith, realize your mortality, finding sorrow for Christ's pain, and vowing repentance for having in whatever way contributed to His death. Embarrassed to wear ashes in public? This then is one way to express your love of Christ publicly – to be the everyday apostle we are each called to be.

May God Bless and keep you, and bring you to His glory – but not too soon!

Lord, may I wear the ashes of penitence with dignity and pride. Let me hold my head high, letting others know that my full commitment is to live in Your embrace and love.

C-4 Question: Why does it always seem as if we're being asked for money? Isn't the church supposed to feed our spiritual needs – not keep hitting us for donation after donation?

Answer: Our duty to support the parish is often overlooked by some. The work of the church, worldwide, is to spread the Gospel, and to nurture God's people – both spiritually and physically. From the beginning of covenant history, God has always insisted that believers contribute from their absolute best – produce, livestock or riches. *(Today the Church asks you to share your time, your talent or your treasure.)* God's requirement has been "tenthing" (old English term) , or giving back to Him at least one-tenth of our wealth – a practice we now call "tithing". Unlike many denominations, the Catholic Church allows you to determine how much you can afford, rather than mandating tithing. How much are our homes, cars, possessions worth these days?

How much do we have in income? How much do we have available in excess of our basic daily needs? How much do we spend on "*nice-to-have*" stuff? Do we throw a few bucks at a time into the collection plate – money we can easily spare, that won't actually cause us any real distress?

Did you know: Over 1 billion people live on less than $1 per day, and that half of the world's population lives on less than $2 per day? Over 800 million people go to bed hungry every day?

The three richest people in the world control more wealth than all 600 million people living in the world's poorest countries?

Yes, the parish has daily needs for money to keep the campus maintained, staffed and usable by all of us. But we could do so much more if Catholics could re-discover tithing instead of "tipping"! There will always be definite needs for capital to replace or improve dilapidated buildings and to expand church facilities. There will also be a time when God asks us whether or not we shared of ourselves to feed His hungry, to house His poor, to heal His sick, to help spread His good news in remote parts of the world, to buy books for children or to help fight for social justice or right-to-life issues. I've never known a priest or pastor who didn't loathe having to beg parishioners for money, but it seems an absolute necessity if we are to survive as God's family or as Christians. The future of our beloved church depends on support from its members, yet each week the parish collection seems to fall well short of its potential. Though there certainly are generous parishioners, each of us might prayerfully take another look at our obligations as members of Christ's church.

Dear Lord, I know that you have no need of my money, but help me to always realize that Your church on earth has as much need for monetary support as does my own family. This is, after all, my second home, and a special place for us to come together to worship You. In order that your church continues to grow and to nourish others as You would wish, let me give freely and from a loving and generous heart, not simply from my excess.

C-5 Question: My friend says I shouldn't ever call my priest "Father". Why not?

Answer: Many non-Catholics think we are disobeying Jesus' instruction in Matt 23:9 to "call no man father" when we give that title to our spiritual leaders. Looking around the bible shows how ridiculous this interpretation is. Jesus was telling us to never replace God as the focus of our adoration, since He is indeed our Heavenly Father. The word, when used in an earthly sense to give honor to a parent or a priest, has no intent of dishonoring God. Jesus, Saint Paul and Saint Stephen use the term freely, referring to the responsibility our spiritual leaders have of bringing new life to our souls, and of protecting us from evil influences. How much more "fatherly" could they be?

Priests go through years and years of dedicated study, get degrees in theology and associated majors, and choose to serve all of us without much material reward. Most are not only college graduates, but many have master's and doctoral degrees as well. Shouldn't we be willing to give them our love and support, and show we recognize their special gift to us by calling them Father? If you need biblical references, see Paul's letters 1 Co 4:14, 1 Th 2:11 and Tit 1:4, among many others. I think God understands how we cherish our priests and smiles as we call his special servants by a term of warmth. It is, after all a sign of respect and love, simply a title they have earned through hard work and devotion to the Father above.

Father in heaven, hallowed indeed is your name before all of creation. Continue to support the priesthood of your church in all things, to guide their hearts and teachings, to give them comfort when lonely, to give them energy when exhausted, and your love when discouraged.

Increase their numbers, O Lord, that their labors may be ever more fruitful. In your name, then, we pray.

C-6 Question: I know about the one-hour fast from food I need to observe before receiving the Eucharist, but does that include other things like medicine?

Answer: Well, I could pull the usual mature person's response – "*Why, our fast used to be so long*", etc., but that's sort of like the old stories about having to walk to school in deep snow, 5 miles, uphill in both directions. The Church simply wants us to stop a moment, reflect and prepare for the wonderful gift that waits for us at mass. We should be aware the Jesus will actually be visiting our body, and missing a bit of breakfast is the very least we can do.

The fasting rule is meant to include actual food items, (including gum), Those things which are consumed for other reasons, such as pills and medications, even vitamins, do not prevent us from receiving the sacrament of Holy Communion. Water, of course, is always allowed.

Per the USCCB (United States Council of Catholic Bishops)– "We are encouraged to receive Communion devoutly and frequently. In order to be properly disposed to receive Communion, participants should not be conscious of grave sin ***and normally should have fasted for one hour.***" (note also, that this one hour means up to the actual reception of the Eucharist)

That said, - why do I feel respect for and understanding of the Real Presence in the Eucharist is fading away somehow? This is the very center of the religion that Jesus founded – His Body and Blood promised to us until He comes again. The many variations of “Christianity” that have sprung up in recent times don’t necessarily have that most critical element – Jesus as true Eucharist! As an extraordinary minister of the Eucharist, I shudder when I hold the host; quake when I serve from the chalice, and positively cower when I visit the tabernacle. How can I presume to serve communion? Like every one of us, I am only a saint-in-training, subject to all the common failings of mankind. Yet, each Eucharistic minister feels exactly the same way, and must.... because we love Christ and are so honored to be able to serve Him. A one-hour fast? Bah!... I remember when I was only a pup ....

Your love, O Lord, surrounds me at mass, at times of solitude and prayer, in the despair I feel in the dark of night, and when I am surrounded by my Catholic family. Help me know and feel your presence, that my courage and commitment will not fail.

C-7 Question: I keep seeing the priests wearing different colors of vestments. Is there a reason for that?

Answer: The colors can be a little confusing, but certainly follow a reasonable pattern. First, you should understand that the Church Calendar starts each year with the season of Advent, which starts on the last Sunday of November each year, on the feast of Christ the

King. The Church year, of course, ends the last day before the next Advent starts, much different from that of the rest of the world. Advent brings us into the color *violet (purple),* used to signify repentance, sorrow and self-examination. Other seasonal colors used are: *Red* - on Pentecost, feasts of the Holy Spirit, and to mark the feast-days of martyrs (signifying the blood they shed for faith.) *White* - (for celebration), used now for funerals, weddings, Baptism, and other major feasts of Our Lady, the Saints and of our Lord. *Gold* - sometimes used for very solemn feasts of Our Lord. *Rose* (the color reserved for the mightiest royalty, telling us of the coming of Jesus either at Christmas or through the Resurrection) – usually used only on the 4th Sunday of Lent and the 3rd Sunday of Advent . *Violet again* – worn during the season of Lent. *Black* – (extreme sorrow), seldom seen now, but formerly worn at funerals. (white has replaced it since funerals should be a celebration of life triumphs and passing on to glory). *Green* – the most common, is worn between seasons throughout of the year, when there is no established special feast. These "green" periods of the Church Season are called "*Ordinary Time*". The name itself simply comes from the term *tempus ordo*, meaning numbered time. Each week in Ordinary Time is sequentially numbered for identity. (This lets those priests with an Irish heritage feel right at home!)

However, none of this really need cause you deep concern. Just celebrate a joyful Eucharist at each Mass you attend, regardless of the color of vestments worn. If you want to know which to expect, though, the dates on the yearly calendar probably issued by your parish during December are all coded with the right color. If your parish doesn't have one, find a good Catholic bookstore or online supplier and get a new calendar to decorate your wall with timely reminders of faith.

May the God of all creation, who lives beyond time and without limit, show you the goodness you can share by loving each person you encounter.

<u>C-8 QUESTION:</u> I notice the church slowly getting noisier and noisier? Why?

<u>ANSWER</u>: I've had a couple of people mention this to me, and some who have even shopped for quieter parishes. The reverent hush that characterized Catholic churches, honoring the presence of Christ and letting us commune quietly with God, seems to have gone by the wayside. There's kind of a split feeling about having a wonderful fellowship with other parishioners, and those who come seeking a quiet and sacred space where they can talk to God without distraction. Maybe we can find a middle ground where we share our joy about being around friends and faith, and yet respect those who are trying to concentrate in a peaceful setting. We might even need to rekindle our awe about being in the very real presence of our Creator.

As we share our joy with others, let us be mindful that there are those who are distracted by our noise, so let us keep it to spiritual exchange, and with quiet dignity. But – "*How do you think the Dodgers are going to do today*?", well- maybe there's a better place for that!

Forgive us our exuberance, O Lord, as we meet joyfully in fellowship with others of our family in the embrace of your sacred space. We mean you no lack of respect, instead glorying in your presence within our circle. Help us remember that others are watching and judging our actions, and our joy is not intended to ever cause you harm. Thank you for allowing us the life to be here, and the friends to share our journey.

C-9 Question: Just what makes us as Catholics different from other Christian faiths?

Answer: We can only touch on this a bit, but let's start by pointing out that, as people of good character, trying to live as God would want, we have a tremendous amount in common with most of the other 40,000+ Christian congregations. We need to continue searching for more understanding, common ground and re-unity, and to realize that God is the only one who can judge who is worthy of salvation.

But….we trace back to being the one church started by Jesus. Our founding members wrote the New Testament of the Bible, copied it by hand through endless generations, guarded it with the lives of martyrs and monks, and preserved it intact for over 1500 years. Our popes, in a hands-on unbroken line back to Peter, give us a continuity of faith and beliefs that can't be found in any other church. We have 2,000 years of wisdom, tradition and scholarship stored up to keep us completely in tune with God's word and with each other around the globe. We treasure those who have gone before us for their faith-filled lives and to whom we remain connected through the "communion of saints."

We have weaknesses, though. As a group, we fail "Communal Singing-101"; take poor responsibility for church support through the collection plate and haven't really committed to a continuing personal growth in knowledge and faith. We haven't gotten comfortable with bible study, nor always fully shared our religious convictions with family and friends. The wonderful sacrifice of the Mass - rich in history and symbolism – is seldom really appreciated by the average parishioner. We often don't feel capable of defending our beliefs if challenged. Is any of this *you*?

We are also a church of majesty, ceremony and liturgy. We are the church of miracles. We are a church of sacramentals, such as rosaries, statues, prayer cards, stations of the cross, and sacred art – all symbols designed to keep us focused on our basic beliefs. We revere Mary as the Mother of Jesus and as our personal spiritual mother. We are a church of "smells and bells" – incense, baptismal fonts, and sacraments. The opportunity to confess our sins to God through a priest, relieving guilt, makes us one of the best-adjusted groups in the world. Most importantly, though, we are a church which has a real presence of Christ, hidden in the Eucharistic bread and wine. We are a church with continuity and unity; with history, tradition and beliefs that keep us close to God.

I love this faith!

C-10 QUESTION: Why do Catholics kneel in front of plaster statues and ask them to pray to God on their behalf. Why can't you just pray directly to God?

ANSWER: Yes, this seems to be a hot topic for pastors of other faiths to point out as one of our "failings". The answer involves several basic Christian beliefs –

One: We are all members of the Communion of Saints, in which there is a continuity of living in the Body of Christ, whether our bodies have entered the recall phase or not. Thus, those who have gone before us and now live triumphantly in God's presence still have a connection with the believers now living.

Two: We are fully aware that the statues, prayer cards, pictures – whatever – that show us a representation of these saints – these are nothing but plaster, paint and paper. They are only there to remind us of our heroes, who have gone before us in faith, and whose strength of spirit and Christian accomplishments inspire us to follow in their footsteps. Just like a baseball card showing Babe Ruth (shows how much older I am) inspires a Little Leaguer to try a little harder, so too we use symbols like statues and pictures to bolster our own spirituality.

Three: Just as all Christians (including those same pastors) have, at one time or another, asked others to pray for them during a time of great need (bypass surgery, the loss of a loved one, etc.), we feel that when we are united in prayer there is more strength and urgency to our petitions. Sure, we continue to pray directly to God ourselves. But... my Mom prayed for me throughout her life, and – believing completely that she has found a home with God – I have confidence that I can continue to ask her to join me as I ask for God's help.

Four: We (hopefully) understand that all prayers are made directly to God, whose power, love and understanding are immeasurable. We also tend to hope that saints (anybody who has been admitted to Heaven) might join in our petition if asked, and that their voices might ring very clearly in God's ears, as they are no longer tainted by earthly faults.

Five: There are undoubtedly a number of Catholics within our billion and a half members who really don't understand these principles when praying before a symbolic statue or picture, and these need to be helped to understand the real, limited purpose of using prayer images. When the Ten Commandments tell us to raise no graven images, all Christians should understand that we are never to raise false gods in adoration – remaining faithful to the one, true Creator. Respecting our "heroes", however, whose faith in that same one God was awesome, simply helps us focus our adoration and spiritual growth in the right direction.

Oh you holy ones who have triumphed here on earth and joined God's adoring throngs in Heaven, look on our weakness and confusion. Help us by your example, and please join with us as we implore God to grant our sincere prayers, but – of course – only as He sees fit.

C-11 Question: I consider a plain cross to be the symbol of Christianity. Why do Catholics use one with a figure of Jesus on it?

Answer: It took several years after the death of Jesus for Christians to start using the cross as a symbol of faith, though the apostles were telling followers to "sign themselves with God's mark" on the forehead well before that. The more intricate crosses soon included a figure of the Savior (though, in the beginning, usually a "resurrection" image), and many were made with very stubby arms on the cross itself so it could be hidden up a sleeve during periods of persecution. Many protestant faiths now point to the plain cross as a symbol of Christ's *triumph over death*, with an empty cross representing a resurrected Jesus. Some also think that a crucifix (a cross with a realistic "cruciform" figure of Jesus on it) is distasteful, and may distress children.

Both types of crosses are wonderful faith expressions, but Catholic Christians prefer the crucifix because it is more importantly a symbol of Christ's sacrifice become a *triumph over sin*, opening the way to eternal life. Lifelike crucifixes have been used for over a thousand years, so they are nothing new. We are all strongly reminded when seeing a "suffering savior" that our weakness and sins personally caused His agony, and we thank Jesus every day for His sacrifice. Children can easily be shown that the crucifix is a symbol of God's love – not of sorrow and death – but of eternal life!

Either way – with cross or crucifix – be proud to display and carry this vivid reminder that our salvation was bought through divine sacrifice. Also remember that we share daily in Christ's burden ourselves. By marking ourselves often with the "sign of the cross" and displaying the crucifix openly and proudly, we bring Jesus into our hearts and homes.

In the name of the Father, and of the Son, and of the Holy Spirit, Amen!

C-12 Question: What makes a saint?

Answer: That is a bit tough to answer. Nothing at all "makes" a saint. A saint is anybody who has attained an eternal reward in God's kingdom. That said, there are untold millions who have done so, but there are some outstanding people who we recognize for having provided an example of spiritual goodness while living on earth. These we sometimes honor with statues, holy cards and the like, which merely remind us of that goodness, and encourages us to emulate their spiritual success.

Now, for the Church to officially declare a person to be a saint, there are many rigorous, extensive and exacting requirements, so that the Church is not proven foolish or mistaken when giving their final validation. Each case is individual, and many of the older "saints" were simply given that designation by those who lived in admiration of them. Grandfathered in, sort of, and most of those came from the ranks of martyrs, who had given their lives in defense of their faith. More modern investigations are very stringent, including endless review of their lives, interrogations of friends and family, and finally – there must have been at least two instances of reliably recorded "miracles", which occurred by God's grace through the intercession of the deceased. These would include anything that could not have happened without God's direct intervention, done to prove His delight in the spirituality and goodness of the person being investigated.

C-13 Question: What are deacons? Are they church elders, or a church council?

Answer: No, the term deacon has been returned to the lexicon of the Church fairly recently – basically in the 1980s. The Second Vatican Council, in noting the shortage of priests, tried to alleviate the situation by re-establishing the position of deacon, which existed from the earliest days of the church, but had been gradually discontinued through the centuries.

The Permanent Deaconate is an ordained ministry, to be of service to the priesthood and the parish. Deacons may baptize, officiate at marriages and funerals, preach and teach, assist at mass, conduct classes, and perform other duties which help a parish run smoothly. Deacons may not hear confessions nor consecrate the sacred species at mass. Deacons may be married, in which case the wife also goes through the 4 or 5 year training alongside her partner, though she is not permitted to undergo ordination. Should a deacon lose his current wife, he is not permitted to remarry. He is bound by a vow of obedience to the local bishop – the ordinary of the diocese.

The first deacons were chosen from among Christ's followers soon after his death, resurrection and ascension into heaven. The original 12 were finding it difficult to spread the religion while also attending to the more mundane aspects of life such as cooking, cleaning, purchasing life's necessities and distributing food, clothing and money among the needy. Seven men were chosen by lot to be of service to the community. The very first of those was Saint Stephen, who also quickly became our very first martyr. The others were Philip, Prochorus, Nicanor, Timon, Parmenas and Nicholas of Antioch. (Acts 6:5) These great men of service became the model for the current rank of the Permanent Deaconate.

Thank you, my God, for bringing the gifts and holiness of these special people into your ranks of the ordained. Bless them and their families, that they may continue to be valued protectors and servants of your flock.

C-14 Question: Where can we get more information about Church beliefs, practices and how I fit into all of that?

Answer: For children the best sources are informed parents who raise informed and enthused children. Next would be for them to attend Catholic schools, which are excellent academically and spiritually. Early solid formation in faith is extremely important, but sadly is often unavailable.

For adults, the Catechism of the Catholic Church, revised by Pope John Paul II in 1992 contains everything you need to know about your obligations in faith, the history and beliefs of the Church, etc. This revision is fairly readable, and should be present in every Catholic's library. It may be purchased from Christian book stores, online or from parish sources.

The 1983 Code of Canon Law is the list of Church laws under which the organization operates. It is an extensive, though somewhat difficult to peruse, source of Catholic regulations. It is used by canon lawyers, appearing before courts of canon law (tribunals), representing members of the congregation as counselors or as prosecutors. Again, a copy of Canon Law may be downloaded from the internet fairly easily, though it would print to almost 400 pages.

The USCCB, the United States Council of Catholic Bishops, is an organization composed of all bishops in the States. It deals with the Vatican on behalf of all dioceses within its jurisdiction, and also publishes a vast amount of data to those who choose to explore its website (usccb.org) or its files. The USCCB is a great resource for all Catholics.

The GIRM, the General Instruction of the Roman Missal, (usually pronounced "germ") instructs our clerics in how to conduct masses, the sacraments and other liturgies. It can be an interesting source of more information.

Beyond that, there is a relatively infinite amount of printed or audio material available at libraries or bookstores about Catholicism. One I've found to be a very good introductory manual of basic Catholicism is "*The Complete Idiots Guide to Understanding Catholicsm*", by Bob O'Gorman and Mary Faulkner. (yes, I'm serious!) Very reader friendly and informative.

If you want to know a book is accepted as authoritative, be sure to look on the back of the title page, for the terms *Nihil Obstat* (I found nothing to object about) and *Imprimatur* (Let this be printed). These are statements by various bishops, representing the authority of the Church, that the contents do not contradict the beliefs of the Catholic Church. It doesn't in any way, of course, guarantee that the contents are well-written, easy to understand, clever, complete or fun to peruse.

Also, become a "joiner" of prayer groups, bible studies, fraternal organizations, etc., and take every opportunity to keep your faith alive and growing in your own parish.

"Your journey is ever upward, often fraught with potholes and detours, but you will overcome all difficulties and enjoy many joys and triumphs along the way if you but put all your trust in me", says your Savior, Jesus the Christ.

C-15 Question: I think I'd like to convert to Catholicism, but why do I have to go through some program like the RCIA (Rite of Christian Initiation for Adults) first?

Answer: Every person's experience of religion and faith has been different. Church leaders want to be sure that participants understand the history, dogma and practices of the Catholic faith. Without that, there can be only confusion and rejection of our practices and liturgies. We have 2000 years of fairly confusing history, and many – often misunderstood – practices, so to make sure that you truly enjoy your new faith and embrace it wholeheartedly, we would like you to have a chance to become familiar with the intricacies inherent in it. This is not to be something that limits or rejects your participation in Catholicism, but merely expands your knowledge so that your experience becomes awesome. Be certain that your being in our pews is a true coming home, and that should start immediately. We are your new family. Our sacraments, especially those of initiation (beginning): Baptism, Confirmation, Reconciliation and Communion, will prepare you for a much fuller participation and understanding of who and what we are.

You are indeed a special person, elevated through Baptism to stand with the Almighty as His child. Your pledge to avoid Satan and all His works will keep you safely on the right course through life. Never despair of God's endless love, His compassion and care.

C-16 Question: I hear of people getting involved in some type of prayer called a novena. What is that?

Answer: There is and always has been a practice in the church to devote special prayers directed to a particular saint or to the Virgin Mary, under any particular guise or title, and for a particular purpose. The seeker who prays asks for the intercession of that saint, etc., hoping that they will add their sanctified requests to God to our own, that we may ask for His blessings and graces in response to our petition.

Remember that we never pray to any saint asking that they use their own power to help us, but rather pray through their special nature as saved, sanctified souls - and to Almighty God.

These prayers sometimes came to be sequential and repetitive, done on nine successive days. These may be public or private entreaties, and can be quite formal or very informal. Public novenas intended for use by church members require written formulas and the *Imprimatur, the Nihil Obstat* and the *Imprimi Potest* – the validation by recognized church authorities.

"How often must I pray to You, my God? How often should I offer you my adoration, my love and my devotion?" And He answers, "Well, just how often do I give you the gift of another breath, my child?"

C – 17 QUESTION I know the main altar at church represents the "table of sacrifice" of Jesus, as well as the "table of the Last Supper". Is there anything else up there important?

ANSWER: I assume you mean besides the main crucifix, the altar candles and the ambo (podium of proclamation of the Gospel) – all of which are mandated by Canon Law and the General Instructions of the Roman Missal.

About all that is left would be the credence table. An ancient custom in royal courts was that a taster, seated at another table, would test food for the presence of poisons before it was presented to the king, bishop, etc. Food which did not kill the taster was then felt to have proved itself – to be believable for consumption. The table was thus called the table of belief, or "tabla credens".

Each altar still has a table of credence upon which rest the "foods" that will become the Body and Blood of Christ until the priest brings them forth to the main altar. It also usually stores extra chalices and other implements of the mass, keeping them pure and unsullied until needed.

Lord, let me always look beyond the trappings of faith, to find the true heart and soul of your religion, and to find there my own salvation.

C -18 QUESTION Is there any reason for having people bring the unconsecrated hosts and wine to the altar during mass?

ANSWER: Yes, there sure is. We, the body of Christ, His "church" present our gifts which will later be consecrated into His physical body – the Body and Blood of Christ by the priest during mass. Our gifts have always been an important event, though in past centuries they could be less than ideal. Homemade wine and bread were often of poor quality, not suited for consecration. Indeed, the habit of watering down undrinkable wine became a norm that we still honor today, by adding a few drops of water to the wine before the elevation. We also, by doing so, are remembering that when Christ was pierced on the cross by a spear, what came forth was a combination of blood and water. And thus we recognize that the pleural fluid that surrounded the heart proved the true death of our savior, and we symbolically recombine those two elements in the main chalice.

So the Church now takes our donations of money and purchases suitable materials to be consecrated during mass, but we still participate by bringing these forward to the priest during the "presentation of the gifts" – our gifts still become the Body and Blood of Jesus.

C – 19 QUESTION I've figured out that the mass vestments signify by color the seasons of the Church, or the celebration of saints, martyrs, etc. Can you tell me, though, what these are called:

ANSWER: These days that's an easier question to answer that it had been 20, 30 or 40 years ago. All of the ceremonial attire used by priests reflect that worn by ancient Jewish clergy, and that worn by upper class Romans of earlier times. These have all evolved during the centuries, and were simplified by decisions made during the Second Vatican Council (1963-1965). Though priests may wear normal clothing during non-clerical times, they may also wear dark clothing with a square "Roman" collar. If they choose to wear a cassock, as many altar servers do, this would be a black, form-fitting upper garment with a Roman collar, and an open lower hem, or skirt. This is worn over regular clothing. During mass, a priest normally wears an alb over normal clothing. Alb means "white", and signifies the purity of the wearer who places himself "in situ Christu" – in Christ's place – at mass. Over this he may or may not wear a stole around his neck, hanging down to around knee high, the sign of his ordained office. Over the alb, in any case, would be the chasuble, which you have noted to be of a color indicating a season or the church or a special event.

Deacons, a relatively new re-introduction to Catholic clergy (mid-1980's) are an ordained ministry. Their badge of office is a stole which angles across their chest from right shoulder to about left knee. They often simply wear the stole over a white alb during mass, but are also authorized to wear a "dalmatic", a chasuble which closely resembles one worn by the presider, but which has two widely-spaced vertical stripes from shoulder to hem.

Walking into one of your churches Lord, is like walking into my own home. I know that here I belong, and that here my beloved is ready to love and nourish me.

C – 20 QUESTION: I've heard non-Catholics we try to sacrifice Jesus at each mass, when he only had one blood-sacrifice for forgiveness of our sins. Are they right?

ANSWER: Well, they are right that the sacrifice on the cross, earned with the pain, suffering and blood of the Messiah, was only necessary once. So, do we sacrifice Him again at each mass? No – we simply tie into the existence of that sacrifice, allowing it to be present to us in a new and special way. It is not the non-bloody sacrifice some call it. It is the original, which still exists in the universe, outside of time and space, and cannot ever be repeated. Be advised that we also are virtually seated with the Apostles at the Last Supper, as we also, as Jesus commanded, bless and consecrate the species of ordinary bread and wine into His Body and Blood. Again, not a new occurrence, but simply allowing it to continue as the Church He founded expands. Both of these events are one-time, all sufficient events which continue at God's desire and command.

I shudder my Jesus, to be reminded so often of your great love and sacrifice, and I am consoled to always find you waiting lovingly at the table of spiritual hope .

C – 21 QUESTION: Whose testimony do we use to validate the Real Presence in the Eucharist? Is it only from the scriptures?

ANSWER: Of course we base that belief solidly on scripture, and the events at the Last Supper. But we also note that the Apostles and all early evangelists held with the truth of the presence of Christ in the consecrated species of bread and wine. Every source, every scholar, every member of the clergy, every pontiff, every Christian authority attested to that same truth for over 15 centuries without pause.

St. Cyril (340 AD) wrote, "Do not, therefore, regard the wine and the bread as merely that, for they are, according to the declaration of the Master, the Body and Blood of Christ."

St. Justin Martyr (about 150 AD) at the request of the Roman Emperor to explain the Eucharist to him reported, "We call this food the Eucharist, and no one else is permitted to partake of it, except one who believes our teaching to be true. For not as common bread nor common drink do we receive these, but since Jesus Christ our Savior was made incarnate by the Word of God and had both flesh and blood for our salvation, so too, as we have been taught, the food which has been made into the Eucharist and by the change of which our blood and body are nourished, is both the flesh and the blood of that incarnated Jesus."

St. Ignatius of Antioch, (about 105 AD) stated in various letters to the faithful, that all must be condemned as heretics any who claimed that the Body and Blood was not present in the Eucharist, and further stated, "I desire the bread of God, which is the Flesh of Jesus Christ … and for drink I desire His Blood, which is love incorruptible."

Even Martin Luther, though he found fault with some aspects of Catholicism, always expressed a deep belief in the Real Presence of

Christ in the Eucharist. He also observed that from the very foundations of Christianity there had never been any question that this was an unalterable truth.

I ache to come home Lord. Here there is such sadness, such violence, such pain and sorrow. But as you continually remind me, there is also such beauty, such love, such hope and such a great bonding of your worldwide family, that I am comforted. I will be patient, then, until I am called to you when my earthly time is over, and I am eager for your embrace!

C-22 QUESTION: When the Blessed Sacrament is openly displayed in a monstrance, why are there so few adorers these days?

ANSWER: That's a very good question! If the displayed host is actually the Body of the Creator of the Universe, and our personal savior, why do we not pay it more attention? In previous years we had a more deeply ingrained respect and awe of the host. Liturgies such as Benediction were much more common. We genuflected on both knees in the presence of the host. The cope (liturgical cape) was used to prevent the priest's hands from touching even the monstrance when it was being moved. A common practice for special times included an around-the-clock 40 hours devotion before the displayed host. Now, we have somehow started to take the Eucharist with much less awe, and more casualness. That appears at communion time when the congregation comes up almost as one, poorly prepared and poorly clothed - seldom displaying much respect. Very few parishes are allowed to set up an adoration chapel, unless they can assure the bishop there will be someone in attendance 24/7. It seems sad, and certainly a sign of the times that we treat the Body of Christ with such a poor display of reverence and awe.

My Lord, please forgive us for taking your precious Body for granted. Help us to know you as our savior and creator, to respect you as an awesome God, and to want to always be in your presence, on earth and eventually in Heaven.

CHAPTER D - THE BLESSED VIRGIN

D-1 QUESTION: I keep seeing different names and titles such as Our Lady of Fatima, Our Lady of Guadalupe, Our Lady of Lourdes, Our Lady of Garabandal, Our Lady of Knock, etc. Are these all referring to the same person? Why are they all dressed differently too?

ANSWER: They certainly are! The Virgin Mary, mother of Jesus, is given the highest respect we can offer to another human, and is often referred to by names that reflect the honor in which we hold her. Some place names identify areas where the Church acknowledges or others believe she has actually appeared as a messenger from her Son, such as Lourdes and Fatima. Others simply arise as we generate loving titles to indicate our respect. Though fully human, Mary certainly deserves a special place of love in the heart of all Christians, regardless of how she is addressed. Out of all time and place, she was chosen from all humanity for the honor of being the perfect mother for the Messiah. How very special she must be!

Of course, you will also see Mary depicted in a variety of beautiful costumes, especially in various locales which wish to honor her with traditional styles and appearances.

Holy Mary, mother of God himself, be our intercessor before His divine throne. Help us, through your example, to become the people He would like us to be, and to bring others to salvation through our own example.

D-2 Question: (from a good friend and parishioner): What is the history of the Rosary, and is the Hail Mary prayer rooted in Biblical sayings?

Answer: I have more complete history of the Rosary printed up, but that takes several pages. Let's simply start with what a wonderful celebration and history of the life of Jesus the Rosary is, as we not only honor His mother, but also meditate on the important aspects of His life and ministry. Catholics aren't the only ones with rosaries in their pockets, either, as some other faiths have found this a very powerful way to pray, and almost every other type of faith uses beads to count prayer. Those who begin the practice of saying a quiet, contemplative rosary sometimes are always amazed at the peace and fulfillment experienced as a result. The very repetitive nature of the prayers brings a deep and thoughtful meditation in faith. In the Rosary, we pray *through* Mary, in honor and love, but *to* Almighty God in thanks and praise.

The rosary is a substitute for an early church practice of reciting the 150 Psalms in monasteries. Unschooled Christians settled for saying 150 *Pater Nosters* (Our Fathers) instead, since they couldn't read the Psalms. Beads gradually came into being to help keep track of the count. The word rosary (*rosarium*, in Latin) means "a garland of roses", and in the 800's AD some monks started praising the Blessed Virgin by including prayers of honor within their devotions.

The "*Hail Mary*" combines the words of the Angel Gabriel who addressed her as: "Hail, (Mary) full of grace! *(*or *Hail, Favored one!)* The Lord is with thee." *(Mk 1:28).* To that was later added the words of Elizabeth at the visitation: *(Mk 1:42*) Blessed art thou among women, and blessed is the fruit of thy womb," The word "Jesus" and the petitions to Mary were added by a Benedictine, Alan de la Roche, in the 1500's.

Regardless, the Rosary is indeed very powerful, and Mary has reportedly asked us recite it daily, especially asking for peace and pledging repentance for sins. The parish center or any Catholic book store has more thorough explanations, and guides to the prayers used.

May Mary keep you warmly in her heart and prayers, and God grant you the graces needed to find eternal salvation!

<u>D-3 Question:</u> I recently heard a preacher say Catholics pray to Mary expecting miracles, and it's wrong to do that. What do you think?

<u>Answer:</u> It's always amazing how our fondness for the Virgin Mary seems to come up negatively so often in non-Catholic sermons. Do we go to places like Lourdes, Fatima or Medjugorje hoping for answers to our prayers? Yup- shore do! Is that wrong? Well, if we understand that we are praying <u>to God</u>, but still giving love and respect to the most perfect human who ever lived – no, it's not wrong. We should revere and copy all of those who have gone before us, strong in spirit and triumphant in grace. As Christians, we know they remain united with us here on Earth. Do I think Jesus or Mary appear to us in the random patterns on French toast or a turtle's belly?...um, let me think…NO!!!

We expect Jesus has a special place in His heart for His earthly mother, Mary. We know she could have been stoned to death for being found with child before marriage, yet agreed to bear the Messiah anyway. She is a great heroine to us all – a role model for us all – and someone who, having been one of us, understands humanity in a special way. When we ask her to lead us to God so we may present our petitions, we show we return her motherly love – but that our faith in God is undiminished by our respect for her.

We can never forget that we only ask Mary to bring our hopes and dreams to her Son; and we know in many cases, miraculous answers can and do come from God as a result. Is it necessary to be in some special place at the time, such as Lourdes or Fatima? Probably not, but it does seem to offer the comfort of a special bond with Mary in an area where she has come to us with messages of peace, hope and love – and where we, with thousands of faith-filled pilgrims, sing in unison to the glory of God.

Heavenly mother, hold us lovingly in your heart, praying to your son Jesus that He may bring us to eternal joy in the presence of Almighty God.

D – 4 QUESTION: Are we as Catholics required to believe in the apparitions of Mary?

ANSWER: Well, no, we are not required to do so by the Church, though it is our privilege to do so if we desire. Marian apparitions such as Fatima, Lourdes, Knock, Guadalupe, etc. have all been thoroughly investigated by Church authorities, and many have been certified as "worthy of belief." These miraculous events have brought us much encouragement and hope, and sound advice from Jesus through his mother Mary. Still, these are not mandatory, doctrinal items which must be accepted and believed by Catholics.

I have walked in the dusty footprints of the very Mother of God. I have spoken to and with her, asking that she help me find my way home to her Son when my time here is over. It is such a comfort to have her presence and advice in my life, much as she nurtured her own Son.

CHAPTER E - GENERAL QUESTIONS

E-1 Question: Why are there so many branches of Christianity?

Answer: I figure that Jesus asks that same question. He came to start one church, not tens of thousands. However, as a Catholic Christian, you can certainly rejoice to be part of the original, one church. We have an unbroken history going back to the time when the Lord himself handed the keys of heaven to Peter. Every other "Christian" faith was established by a human being, for human reasons, at least 1500 years after Christ, and some as late as last Tuesday. Though every faith expression has a potential for establishing good standards of behavior and spirituality for their members, I am personally very proud to be called a Catholic. Still, we might sometimes ask ourselves if we are as knowledgeable, enthused and faith-filled as some of our brethren from different faith expressions. And, we need to remember to let God, who certainly made all people deliberately, and in His image, judge the true worth of each person in the world, and the appropriateness of their method of worshiping Him.

Lord, all Christians and indeed all good people of faith seek you and try to live as you would have us do. Give me the wisdom to see You in every person I encounter, and to judge them not – leaving such to Your compassionate understanding and just review.

E-2 Question: My family moved here from a small town in Oregon a couple of years ago. There we were members of a small parish where we really felt at home, but somehow we still feel like outsiders here at this new parish. How can we fit in better? (anonymous)

Answer: Well, first and foremost, a warm and enthusiastic welcome (somewhat belated) to your new home parish. I know there is a different feel to a larger urban parish than what you might be used to. Coming from a small town myself, where everybody knew you as a friend and neighbor – being lost in a larger group can be disconcerting. My wife and I have been here for years now, though we are outside the geographical area of closer parishes. Some see this as a poor practice called "parish-hopping" but it worked extremely well for us. Sorry if you haven't found that warmth and acceptance yet – but keep looking!

I do know that if you give us a chance by getting very active, you'll soon make loads of good friends. The focus of religion, of course, is always directed toward finding a relationship with God, but the social aspects of "fitting in" and "belonging" can't be ignored. "Church" consists of the Body of Christ, which means all of us who believe, and we need to learn to share our joy and spiritual fervor with everyone else in that body. There are tons of great people sitting in the pews with you who would love to get to know you better. Do whatever you can to become better acquainted; to join ministries; to be open and friendly with others at mass; to sit and gab at the monthly pancake breakfasts; to join in all activities and liturgies, to seek out opportunities like the various bible study classes, etc. We are all called as Christians to bond not only with God, but also with each other – to support and love one another as Jesus has supported and loved us. Again, welcome home!

Jesus, I look around at those who remain strangers to me, knowing that they rest in your heart just as I do. Help me to open myself to them, to make them welcome if they feel awkward, to show them that this parish, and my family and myself are looking forward to becoming their friends and supporters.

E-3 Question: I've heard that only one Christian church was started by Jesus. What about this?

Answer: Well, the following list is interesting info, not intended to criticize any faith expression's beliefs. But…it does illustrate the very human origin of just a few of the thousands of Christian churches, all of whom are offshoots of Catholicism. They have progressively branched and re-branched from each other as individual members disagreed about policy or belief.

Lutheran - Martin Luther, a Catholic monk, in 1517

Anabaptist – Nicholas Storch and Thomas Munzer, in 1521

Church of England – King Henry VIII

(arguing divorce with Pope), in 1534

Presbyterian – John Knox (former Lutheran), in 1560

Congregationalist – Robert Brown, in 1582

Episcopalian – Samuel Seabury – American colonies, 17th century

Mennonite – Menno Simons, 16th century

Amish – Jacob Amman (ex Mennonite) – 17th century

Baptist – John Smyth, Amsterdam, 1606

Dutch Reformed – Michaelis Jones, New York, 1628

Methodist – John & Charles Wesley, England, 1744

Unitarian – Theophilus Lindley, London, 1774

Latter Day Saints (Mormon) – Joseph Smith (age 15), 1829

Church of Christ – combined by Barron Stone and Alexander Campbell from Baptist and Presbyterian origins, in 1836

Seventh Day Adventist, Ellen G. White, 1844

Salvation Army – William Booth, London, 1865

Christian Scientist – Mary Baker Eddy, 1879

Jehovah's Witness – T. Russell – early 1900's

Pentecostal – any of thousands of churches founded within 1900's

Non-Denominational - started in the later 1900's demanding independence from any outside authority

(above information extracted from: ewtn.com/faith/teachings/churb4.htm)

If you are Catholic – Jesus Christ, the Son of God, started your faith just before His death (circa. 33 AD), leaving the Apostle Peter with full authority as our first Pontiff. Our practices, beliefs, authority structure and dogma have not basically changed since that time. Who wrote the New Testament, guarded all Christian teachings and beliefs, suffered persecution, brought Christ's word to the entire known world well before the 1500's?– The Catholic Church, of course! Be sure, be proud!. References: Jn 21:15-17, Mt 16:18-19, Acts 2,1, Tim 3:15

Continue to remind me, O Lord, that your family is not always called Catholic, or Christian, or by any other label. Your goodness shines forth from many eyes, from many faiths, from many lands - and your praises are sung in many languages.

E-4 Question: I've been told that my brown scapular will guarantee salvation. Can it really do that?

Answer: No, not absolutely. Well, let's put it this way…our Lady did promise that those who died wearing her scapular, and who had been faithful to God's teachings would receive her intercession and special prayers to God on their behalf. So the promise is valid, but we are required to do our part.

Let's also clarify what sacramentals (*little sacraments*) are in the first place. While our seven major sacraments allow us to interact directly with God in a very intimate way through the outward signs of water, bread and wine, oil of anointing, etc., sacramentals are very different. Scapulars, rosaries, holy water, statues, oils of anointing, pictures etc., etc., are all just *things*, symbols of faith, blessed for a religious purpose and meant to help us stay aware of our commitment to lives of Christian worth. If they show real power, it is not something inherent within them, but could come only through the exercise of God's will.

The brown scapular is normally worn by a person who submits to the lay associate rules of the Carmelite order, and the scapular itself must be "invested" by an ordained Carmelite priest. These have a very wide acceptance, and even papal recognition, but are still bound by the limitations above.

My God, I know there is indeed life within your sacraments, and love and support. Help me to become better and more in tune with your promises through each sacrament of which I partake.

E-5 Question: Just when and where did the Catholic Church get its name?

Answer: Well, the first recorded instance that we still have access to of the word "catholic" (*kataholos* in the original Greek) is found in the Letter to the Smymeans written by Ignatius of Antioch in 110 AD. Many other very early writings include the word, simply meant originally to imply "universal". Christ's church started out being called "*The Way*", distinguished by the concept of a single God to be worshiped by the entire world. At the time, most religions honored local "gods", different in each town, province or country. The concept of only one God, a God who created the entire universe, to be universally worshipped throughout the world, was a staggering one. The term "catholic" gradually became the common way to identify this wonderful religion, and eventually the actual, formal name of "*the Catholic Church*".

The universality of the Catholic Church is astonishing to me, my God. You have allowed me to feel at home in faith wherever in the world I happen to be.

E-6 Question: I understand that some Catholics expect to buy their way into heaven through "good works". Is this true?

Answer: This is a common misconception, and certainly not true. As with all mainstream Christian groups, Catholics understand that Christ bought our salvation through the pain and sorrow of His death. No matter how many good works we do, we can't earn salvation for ourselves, as it has already been "bought" by the only sacrifice great enough to deserve it. Now that eternal life has been earned and offered, however, we are certainly able to turn down our inheritance by dying in a state of serious sin. God's saving grace, accepted in time, gives us a way to come home through the confessional, with repentance and absolution.

Now, good works are definitely expected of any Christian. (see Ephesians 2:10 .. "For we are His workmanship, created in Christ Jesus for good works…..") God has a plan for each of our lives – to be productive and to carry out his plan of salvation. Jesus expects us to continue living in faith and allowing others to see our joy in being His followers. Our good works should include studying our religion, trying to advance in spirituality, participating in church ministries, reaching out to the unfortunate, giving of our resources to church and other worthy needs, willingly testifying to our beliefs publicly and within our families and circles of friends, and any other way that keeps our Christianity alive and tuned-up.

God's church is a collection of all believers, certainly not just Catholics, and I'm sure He rejoices in us as we grow more mature in faith. Acts of mercy, love, charity, compassion and good example are what we are asked to bring to salvation's table. How often should we thank and praise God for this grace?....well, - how often does He grant us the gift of our next breath?

If I could buy my way into Heaven, Lord, with what coin could I pay? Certainly not in the riches of the world, so then it must be only with the riches I hold within me. My love, my compassion for others, my example to them, and my being present wholly and with purity to you, to myself and to all others. I'm willing to pay, Sweet Jesus, but even that coin is inadequate without your sacrifice.

E-7 Question: Why does the Catholic Church have the right to make rules that I'm required to follow - things like not eating meat on Lenten Fridays or fasting before Communion?

Answer: Jesus gave this right when He founded the church, and handed the keys to Peter. *(MT 16: 18-19)* Church leaders are morally responsible for guiding members toward salvation. Sometimes we are best reminded of spiritual truths by being required to follow certain rules or practices. A small penitential act such as abstaining from meat for the six Fridays of Lent makes us more aware that Christ died on Good Friday only because our sins required it. We are being encouraged to cultivate a sorrow for those sins through at least some symbolic penance.

The one-hour communion fast (which has been simplified from the earlier regulation to avoid food or liquids from midnight on) simply reminds us that we will have the privilege of consuming the very Body and Blood of Christ in the Eucharist. This slight nudge to purify our bodies by sacrifice before our intimate encounter with the Lord helps us be more aware of the importance of what we are doing. We follow a Church rule to attend mass on all Sundays and appointed feast days, so we take God's instruction to "Keep holy the Sabbath day" seriously, even if USC and UCLA are having a cross-town battle, or the beach or snow seem to be calling our name! All rules such as these are certainly man-made, and can be changed in ways the Church deems necessary to help develop our sense of the spiritual, and to gain maturity of faith. They rightly result in sin if willfully, knowledgeably and deliberately disobeyed.

Help me to walk away from self-involvement, from insincerity and from selfishness, Lord. Help me come to know you, love you and follow you without thought to my own conceits and interests. Your embrace is all I seek, all I wish to know.

E-8 QUESTION: Why do we as a parish have to belong to this diocese? Can't we be independent of them? (Submitted in the Sunday collection)

ANSWER: Maybe this is a tongue-in-cheek question, but maybe not. I recognize that there have been some changes in the parish and within the Church itself. First answer: No, we are not an independent unit.

However, let me elaborate a little. When Jesus founded the Catholic faith, He set up a structure that exercised His authority through a group of leaders, the Apostles. Thank goodness, that structure has held us together as a unified church for almost 2,000 years, unified in belief, practices, liturgy and prayer. Other faith expressions change and branch off in many different directions, but our doctrines remain steady – because of the uninterrupted influence of church leaders. Today's bishops trace their lineage back to those same Apostles, as well as their right to keep us united in faith. The very ground we stand on, and the buildings we worship in literally belong to the local bishop, who has a responsibility to govern those resources in our best interest. We have a right to express our opinions, but final decisions must rest with him.

There is an organization called the *Old Catholic Church* (Mel Gibson is a faithful member), which broke away from this structure a few years ago in revolt against the reforms of Vatican II. They now own their own parishes, and answer only to their own authority. The Vatican reluctantly recognizes the validity of their sacraments and doctrine (see the Papal document *Dominus Ieusus* published in August 2000), but such separation definitely represents a crack in the unified Body of Christ.

Let me also say that this is a time for healing and examining whether we can obey Jesus' command to "*Love one another as I have loved you*!" Priests cycle through our parish on a regular basis, and it is one of the Bishop's jobs to manage parish staffing in whatever way will stimulate our spiritual growth and maintain the highest level of parish efficiency. We are gifted with a multi-cultural assembly, and we need to find ways to diminish anything that keeps us from becoming fully united in all things "parish", in all things "Christian" – in all things "Catholic". It's time to move away from dissension and anything that distracts from our worship as the true "Church" of Christ.

Lord, guide me into an awareness of your presence within your church, and within each person I encounter on my journey toward you. Hold my hand that I not stumble into spiritual danger, and lead me toward safe pasturage within your sheepfold.

E-11 Question: I see such vigor sometimes in other faiths. Why don't I feel that in my own Catholic faith?

Answer: OK – let's regain the vigor and excitement… starting with you and me! The Catholic faith is so rich in content, tradition, knowledge and history. We have the very real presence of Christ in our Eucharist. We are the church He founded. We wrote the New Testament and guarded it through centuries of struggle. We still have the exact same core beliefs we started with. We aren't subject to change at the whim of some earthly preacher. So why aren't we excited about all that! I really can't tell you why we have gotten so complacent with such riches. Maybe it's time to re-examine our faith lives. Are we singing joyfully during mass or snoring loudly? Do we stop once in a while during our daily lives to have a conversation with God? Are we teaching our children about the wonders of Catholic Christianity? Do we feel knowledgeable enough ourselves? Many of my friends have been away from an active participation in Catholicism at some point in their lives, and each has confessed that coming back was truly a "coming home".

How about going to mass once sometime when you're not obligated, just for heck of it. How about taking 30 seconds at the end of your day to thank God, just for ... well... everything!! Start building that vigor and excitement back into your own faith life, and be sure to share it with friends and neighbors.

God's love and blessings to you at all times. May you never fail to look for the excitement of a realized faith, to thank God for His presence in your life, and may the energy of God shine forth from all you do.

E-12 Question: I keep hearing the term "charismatic" Catholic. What does that mean?

Answer: Big subject to cover, but the Charismatic Renewal started after Vatican II with a hope of bringing more excitement and a rebirth of deep spirituality to the church – and not only the Catholic church. This is an ecumenical movement to regain a deep contact with the Holy Spirit in Christian faith expressions. There was great promise in the early movement, and it endures, yet may not have yet found its fullest promise.

Charisms, for which the movement is named, are those gifts of the Holy Spirit that best mimic the great ones given to the Apostles at Pentecost. Each of us receives these in some measure, especially through Baptism and Confirmation, but they become evident only as we become open to using them. They might include the more visible ones such as the gift of prophecy, of speaking in tongues, or of healing. More common and just as important are the gifts of being a good teacher, a good writer, a good speaker, a peacemaker, an organizer, a compassionate listener, etc. These "charisms" are then your spiritual purpose in life! What has been gifted to you?

The gifts of the Holy Spirit are always given freely to the recipient – but are never to be hoarded for personal benefit or prestige – but always to be aimed outward, to improve others' relationship with God. Perhaps charismatics need to recall that these gifts are to be spent only on others, not kept to themselves.

Fundamentalist or Pentecostal movements have always sought this union with the Holy Spirit, but their outflow of emotion and excitement has found a difficult foothold in more conventional, sedate religions such as Catholicism. When some faiths talk about being "born again", it refers to being "reborn in the Spirit" – or experiencing a "baptism of the Spirit", in which we become filled with the influence of the Holy Spirit by making ourselves fully open to His presence and inspiration. Maybe it's time we invited God's influence, and to look inward to see if we have the potential to share gifts which will enhance His kingdom. You certainly don't have to hunt up a charismatic prayer group to realize your own potential for helping others grow in faith – but, it couldn't hurt either! May God's love shine on all!

May the Holy Spirit find in me a worthy host of his love and guidance.

E-13 Question: A couple of years ago I stopped into St. Patrick's Cathedral in Dublin, Ireland. We were actually almost finished with mass before I realized I wasn't in a Catholic church. Where was I?

Answer: Well, I have to giggle a little, because Darlene and I did exactly the same, except we luckily couldn't get into "mass" because Oxford was holding graduations there at the time. Yes, we think of St. Pat's Cathedral in New York as sort of the bastion of Catholicism, but St. Patrick's, Dublin belongs to the Church of Ireland.

You probably remember that King Henry VIII took over the Catholic Church in England in 1531 because the Pope wouldn't let him divorce Catherine of Aragon. The takeover was extremely bloody, and – now rejecting papal authority – its followers, including Henry, were automatically excommunicated. It became known as the Anglican Church, (Church of England) retaining the characteristics of Roman Catholicism, except that the Archbishop of Canterbury became the spiritual head, and the king (currently the queen) retains overall authority. There are almost 70 million members worldwide, many under related names, including the Episcopal churches of Scotland and the United States, the Church of Ireland, and about 35 others. Together these form the Anglican Communion and are all separate, though agreeing pretty well on beliefs and liturgies. Most recognize the Archbishop of Canterbury as titular head, without necessarily granting him authority over church affairs. The Anglican groups are certainly the closest to us in belief, and we can always hope that God's influence will some day allow us to reunite. In the meantime, sacraments taken in Anglican Communion churches are invalid for Catholics, and the services do not satisfy our requirement of attending Sunday mass.

Remind me, Lord, that you live in many places. That your are where good people gather in your name, regardless of where that is, and that your love abounds in the hearts of all who seek you in truth and faith.

E-14 QUESTION: (Do you think it's possible that aliens exist and are visiting us?

ANSWER: Well, first of all, I'll worry about aliens then next time Mars attacks. But....we exist in a minor galaxy of the universe, surrounded by hundreds of thousands of other solar systems with billions more stars and trillions of planets – what are the chances that God has created life in other locations? I suppose the odds are pretty good we're not alone, but the only thing we know for certain is we are God's children, created for a purpose, asked to love and serve Him, and known and loved individually by Him without limit.

(In the meantime, beam me up, Scotty! The Klingon are coming!)

E-15 Question: What do you think would improve Catholic faith life?

Answer: I suppose there are tons of answers to that question, and I agree that we need to shake up our faith a little. Picking out only a couple of important things, though, I'd have to go with a need for community and for forgiveness.

Christianity has been splintered from the one church Jesus and Peter started 2000 years ago, into over 40,000 variations. I believe they all have a certain value for influencing people's lives in a positive way, but – do I believe they all are equal to the founding religion? – no, I'm afraid not. Why do we split up every time there is a slight disagreement over something? Each of those 40,000 religions has been started by some human, for human reasons – pride, anger, righteousness, greed, envy – or because they truly believe they have found a better way to connect to our Creator. I can't fault those who want a life that spiritually enriches themselves and others, but I do hope we can eventually regain common ground and reconciliation.

Even in our Catholic faith, we see a decline in attendance; in spiritual purity; in commitment and in fundamentals of belief. We need to regain being a family of believers, solidly interlocked with our brothers and sisters around the world. We need to find pride and strength in our church community, so our example of unity will bring back some who have strayed in a different direction, and refocus our own faith. Community!

For forgiveness, look at the great example of the Amish recently when their schoolchildren were attacked and killed– able to find forgiveness in their hearts for the violence done. We ask for God's forgiveness in the *Our Father*, to the extent we forgive others. Can we actually do it? It's terrible how hurt, anger and a lust for revenge damages our own lives, leading to depression, antagonism and a loss of appreciation for life. When we forgive, we don't have to forget, nor lose the lesson we learned from another's betrayal – just let go of the pain! We are hurt by others, and hurt ourselves every time we do something that shames us internally. You really don't need to kiss or buy another car from the same idjit who tricked you into buying that lemon – but you need to let go of the anger. If we can just release the heavy burden of hate, anger and disappointment, at ourselves or others, we can rekindle the joy of Christianity and love again. Forgiveness!

Help me, Lord, to unburden myself of the things that sometimes weigh me down – disappointments, sorrows, hurts and an awareness of my continued sinfulness. Your compassion and forgiveness are such a gift, my God!

E-16 QUESTION: Why are Catholics against celebrating Halloween?

ANSWER: Well, if you're thinking about the warm, fuzzy version of Halloween - kids in cute costumes collecting candy door-to-door – church authorities usually watch with a smile, and probably grab a few goodies for themselves.

However, the history of this date has involved a celebration of death, demonology, witchcraft and human sacrifice in times past. Even the Druids had a harvest festival that would have made your head spin. As the days became darker and shorter in autumn, superstitions arose that the world was slowly coming to an end in the bitter winter days. A lot of wild revelry and sacrifice, together with huge bonfires to keep the dark away seemed to prevent this catastrophe each year, so they kept on doing it every fall. Apparently it worked, since the world is still here. (the Catholic Church overcame most Druidic influence in the 700 and 800s.)

Demon worship and black masses still happen each Halloween, when some believe the veil between this world and the afterworld is stretched to its thinnest the day before the feast of All Souls. (Halloween is just Old English for All Hallows Eve)

So, as long as the fun is innocent, the official Church position these days is to try to ignore the darker aspects of October 31st – though they probably turn a wary eye on some of the little witch or devil costumes. But, on the following day, All Souls, be sure to honor those members of the communion of saints who have gone before us by attending mass and remembering them in your prayers!

(Oh, by the way, I'm going to disguise myself this Halloween as a balding, older gentleman with a beard – should be a real hoot!)

E-17 QUESTION: Why does God permit pain and death if He can prevent it?

ANSWER: There's probably not enough space to really give you a good response, but – basically, ……we are human. Organic beings have a shelf life, though that which is divine within us, our soul, is destined to live eternally. God permits us to live in our natural state, vulnerable to all the ills of the body and mind, and eventually to join

Him after death. There will never be a human understanding of why some are afflicted young or excessively, but it remains a constant human condition nevertheless. God's purposes, plans and very being remain to our meager intelligence a great mystery, to be taken on faith.

I recently came across a nice way to state the obvious. On our memorial plaques there will be two dates – birth and death. But the important element will be the little, insignificant "dash" between those dates. That dash represents all we have been, believed, known, done, acted on. What would our own "dash" represent? Have we improved the place we've lived, the lives of others that we've touched? Have we grown stronger in personality, stronger in faith and stronger in love? Have the tragedies, difficulties, work, discipline, pain and sorrows we've known been allowed to help us develop into beings of worth and stature – or broken us? God permits us – even gifts us – with such trials the way fire tempers steel. Our struggle lets us come to God stronger and purer than those who cannot bear the burden, and who have forgotten that God walks each step of our lives with us and loving us. Hold out your hand to Him. I know that He often walks with us in sorrow, His compassion for our troubles endless.

Bring solace to our suffering hearts, O Lord!

E-18 Question: Why is there such a shortage of priests these days?

Answer: There are bunches of answers to that one. Certainly world economics play a role, as more young people elect to enter a secular career path instead of the one offered by the Church. Certainly our modern emphasis is more on achieving affluence and power than in seeking the quiet peace of a religious life. Certainly the "priestly scandals", actually involving very few clerics, have still tainted the pride and authority of the entire priesthood, lessening the draw to a religious vocation.

However, as I pointed out previously, the decisions of our youth are often dictated by the actions and guidance received from parents. Does your family pray together, eat together, discuss religion and concepts of God together? Do you ever attend mass when you don't "have" to. Does your family ever see the inside of the Adoration Chapel? Does it seem important to start encouraging your child very early to "become successful", to "aim high", to seek positions of power, influence and wealth? Don't we all want doctors, lawyers, professors and scientists to blossom from the family tree? But…is that actually success? When God sends out a quiet call for a vocation to the religious life, are we drowning out that sacred voice with demands for outstanding performance… in Little League, in dance, in school, in life…in all these secular things that really mean so little. God calls our children to be willing to give up worldly things, and to follow Him….to cradle those in need as they would gently tend broken birds… to spend lives of true worth and dedication. Living in community and feeling the peace and satisfaction of being worthy friends of Jesus – these things are truly better than earning another ulcer in the corporate world! Are we, by example and encouragement, letting our children know a religious life is worthy of serious consideration, or are we making sure they don't "abandon" us and our more worldly goals? In forgetting the very real rewards, here and in the afterlife, of the religious life, are we ourselves partly responsible for the decline in vocations?

Your shepherds, O Lord, are in short supply, and your flock is increasingly in danger of becoming stranded or swallowed up by the world's distractions. Send us your dedicated, your wise, your informed and your compassionate, Lord, that they may guide us to your eventual eternal embrace.

E-19 Question: I sometimes hear the term "Doctor of the Church" ... is this a physician or something else?

Answer: The term applies to great teachers through Church history, who are also examples of sanctity and whose influence had been pivotal at some point in history of preserving or building Church principles. The term "doctor" is derived from the Latin word *docere*, which simply means teacher.

There are four who are often pointed out as great leaders in early Church times, including Saint Augustine, Pope Gregory I, Saint Jerome and Saint Ambrose.

Other lists start with Clement of Rome, Ignatius of Antioch, Justin Martyr and Irenaeus of Lyons, beginning from the earliest days of the Church.

Added over the centuries have been over 35 more, including St. Thomas Aquinas, St. Teresa of Avila, St. Catherine of Siena and St.

Therese of Lisieux. The list is not exact, and the process is not well defined, but generally the Congregation for Divine Worship in the Vatican selects worthy individuals for the term "Doctor". These people are often called "Fathers of the Church" for their role in helping the faith to grow and develop, and the list continues to increase.

May your spiritual physicians, Lord, look to my weakness of faith, and help me find and know you better. I pray so often that I may become the person I think you want me to be – have pity on my many faults, and help me develop the love and compassion your saints have demonstrated.

E-20 Question: I've been told that the current Catholic Church has been in apostasy (heresy) since it allowed the Roman Emperor Constantine to dictate the terms of the Council of Nicaea in 325, and no longer can be considered the church Christ started. Was this true?

Answer: Funny, I've heard that said also, and found the premise ridiculous. The pagan emperor embraced a deep belief in the teachings of Jesus when told in a dream to conquer Rome using the symbol of the Christian cross on his men's shields and banners. He won the battle easily, and subsequently made Christianity the official religion of Rome.

Having been told that he only had one chance to be baptized and find forgiveness of sin before death, he elected not to convert until his deathbed, so as to be more certain of salvation as a Christian. He was lucky enough to validate that precarious choice.

At that time, there was very poor organization in the Christian world, with many mistaken beliefs and heresies going on, and little coordination between bishops and other church leaders. Constantine, though officially still a pagan, was disgusted with the situation, and so insisted that all bishops of the world gather at Nicaea to hold a council in the year AD 325, to stamp out false teachings and outright heresy, and to consolidate church beliefs as taught by the original apostles. This they did, and it included revising the Apostle's Creed (becoming then the Nicene Creed) so there would no longer be confusion about the divinity of Christ, the existence of a triune Divinity, and many other aspects of Catholicism. It was a necessary and vital movement to help the church organize and to prevent the spread of false doctrine. Though organized by Constantine, and called to order by the same, the Council of Nicaea was the first official worldwide (at the time) gathering of Christian clergy. It created or validated a solid foundation of Church doctrine, and became the first of 20 additional councils in subsequent centuries. The 2nd Vatican Council, of course, which was held just recently, in the early 1960s, was modeled on same format as the Council of Nicaea.

Constantine had in the process preserved the integrity of the Church, regardless of his status as a Roman Emperor and (temporary) pagan. His heart and his family held only the highest esteem for Christ's church, and to find that his interest in the welfare of that church has been called "the end of Christianity" or the beginning of an "apostate" Catholicism is a great misstatement.

May we all come to understand how the 20 great Councils of the Church have allowed us to remain intact as a religious nation through the centuries. Show our hearts that these convocations of your princes of the church have kept us from heresy, not caused it. Let your bishops continue to guide us as the Holy Spirit dictates, and may their wisdom become the touchstone of our faith.

E-21 Question: I'm a bit confused about the rank of church leaders. Can you help?

Answer: Yes! The rank of leadership in the Catholic Church is a bit upside-down, as the Pontiff, the Pope, considers himself the servant of those under his direction, as do the cardinals, the bishops, etc. in turn. Still, the bishops are the successors to the *Episcopoi,* direct descendants of the twelve apostles. Bishops appoint and consecrate priests to God, laying hands on them to convey their authority directly. They also train and ordain members of the Permanent Deaconate.

(I'll leave out the fryers, monks, abbots, brothers, nuns, etc., who are in a separate class entirely.)

Basically there are only 3 ranks in the public church – deacon, priest and bishop. However, those break down a bit into sub-categories. Some priests (the original term being *presbyters*) having been recognized as being of special importance or of great service, are infrequently raised by a local bishop to the title of *Monsignor* (though that has recently been a rank dropped from the hierarchy by Pope Francis). It is simply an honorary designation, without increase in authority or responsibility.

Bishops, as successors of the Apostles themselves, are the titular heads, the "ordinary" (usual source of authority) of dioceses, a territorial area comprising a group of local parishes under the direction of the local ordinary.

Bishops can be raised to a rank of archbishop, becoming an organizing force for several dioceses, or to be the local ordinary for an extremely large or important territory.

Bishops can be appointed by the Vatican to the rank of Cardinal (first in order) bishops, who then may represent the interests of their local dioceses when the Vatican makes organizational decisions.

Cardinal bishops may be elected to the College of Cardinals, which is a group of men (usually around 120 in number) who offer advice directly to the Pope, and meet in session to elect replacement popes when necessary.

The Pope, or Pontiff of Rome, (which is a layman's casual, friendly nickname for the "Papa" of the church) is simply the Bishop of Rome, the inheritor of the mantle of our first authority, St. Peter. He is considered to be Christ's voice on earth, and as said, the servant of the servants of the people. While he has great authority and influence, he is also responsible to guide and encourage the controlled growth of the church and see to the spiritual and physical welfare of his worldwide flock.

There have been only two instances where a pope has officially spoken "from the chair of Peter", requiring that the entire church accept the truth of a matter. These included the belief that the Blessed Virgin was born without sin (the Immaculate Conception) and that she was taken to Heaven body and soul after death (the Assumption of the Blessed Virgin). Those concepts are more fully explained in another recent Q and A.

Guide us through the words of your Vicar on Earth, the Pontiff of the western Catholic faith. We await his wisdom, that we may know your will.

E-22 Question: I've heard the term "diocesan priest" and also "order priest". What is the difference?

Answer: Diocesan priests are selected, trained and ordained into their priesthood by local bishops, who then keep their services confined to one diocese unless released to the authority of another bishop if requested. They generally take two vows upon ordination – chastity (to remain pure and unmarried), and obedience (to the authority of that bishop.)

Order priests, or members of a religious group are authorized by the Vatican upon request to form a separate identity, if their rules seem acceptable and also to practice a particular *charism* (gift of the Holy Spirit), which becomes their reason for being and their function in life. These gifts can include healing, teaching, missionary work, praying, etc. You have all heard of a few of the many orders, including Franciscan, Dominican, Claretian, Jesuit, Cistercian, Carmelites and so on. These exist outside the authority of local bishops, though cooperation is always expected. Members are not always, or even often, ordained priests. Many are monks, brothers or friars. Some communities live in isolation, seeking a spiritual haven. Most others, however, live and work within the outside world. These men (or women) usually take three vows – Chastity, Poverty, and Obedience (to the head of their particular order.) Their service is often wide ranging, missionary in nature, and very dedicated.

The dedication of your servant priests is truly amazing my Lord. Thank you for your gift to help with our continuing struggle

E-23 Question: What do you think about the priestly scandals?

Answer: Again, I can't completely cover that issue here, but surprisingly I find that the overall effect has been to cleanse the church, reenergize our clergy, take the priesthood as a whole off a pedestal on which we had unwisely placed them, and give us a much more solid church in return. I think that God did a very necessary pruning of the vine, for the overall health of the vineyard. We will recover.

I was in a high-school level seminary for some years, hoping to become a missionary to Africa, but found that the isolation was difficult. I eventually left to become a family man, and have not regretted the decision at all.

We were prohibited from being alone with any woman other than mother or sister, required to remove pictures of females from the magazines that cluttered our lounges, to listen only to male singers on the radio, etc. Somehow that seemed a poor policy, potentially creating people with an immature sexuality. Then we expect priests to live in absolute chastity for the rest of their existence, forsaking a right to enjoy normal families and the partnership of a loving wife. It seems a bit presumptuous to think that under those conditions all things remain completely normal, or that sexual immaturity is not a common result.

I marvel at those who stayed the course and have turned that isolation into a virtue – who find sustenance in being shepherds to flocks of great people. How I admire the hundreds of giving, spiritual and compassionate men of God I have known in my life!

The incidence of abuse among Catholic priests is approximately around 1%, much less than that of the general population. About 5% of people become abusers; parents, friends, neighbors or other relatives who take advantage of positions of authority to permanently damage others. Still, any figure is unforgiveable. For decades, bishops were "guaranteed" by psychologists that priests could be cured, and such priests were often thrust back into society and, unfortunately, places of opportunity. This is not a homosexual issue, nor a heterosexual one – but an abuse of power, sometimes by sexually immature men. Whatever the cause, whenever it occurs, it painfully violates the absolute trust we traditionally grant priests.

It is a great thing for the health of the church that we can now deal openly with whatever problem might still exist. Those who have little self-control or who seem untrustworthy are no longer trained in seminaries nor ordained as priests. Deep psychological study is given each candidate, and many are rejected. Older men with problems have been weeded out, laicized, or even excommunicated. Every new priest goes through intensive counseling and studies human psychology extensively during their time in seminary. There unfortunately will never be a time when all weakness can be erased from mankind, but the Catholic Church has undergone a period of renewal that leaves it a much better place. The vine has been pruned, indeed.

Catholics no longer silently tolerate the existence of abusing clergy, and many preventive measures are also now in place to protect the innocent, whether those innocents happen to be wrongly treated children or even wrongly accused priests.

Bring peace to your people, my God. Show us that your emissaries are again worthy of trust, but remind us always that they are not a separate race of people, simply ordinary but dedicated men who sacrifice to serve. Bring new life to our seminaries, and revitalize the spirits of discouraged priests.

E-24 Question: What are religious cults?

Answer: The short version is that cults are formed around the opinions and direction of one strong personality figure, a person whose pride makes acceptance of his absolute viewpoints mandatory, especially as regards religion. Most cult leaders say they have an authority direct from God to teach, to lead, to punish and coerce. (think Jamestown, Ruby Ridge, Waco and many others) The resultant religious beliefs and actions may sometimes be benign or but are more likely to be wildly radical, skewed totally away from God's plan for mankind.

A true religion is formed around the concept of the Almighty, a creator, a lover, a divine and holy entity. That is the strong personality we choose to follow, sometimes allowing others to help us find ways to seek a relationship with the divine.

Lord, let me hear your quiet and loving voice when I need spiritual guidance. I will follow in your footsteps, and in those of your apostles, and I offer my feeble assistance wherever you have need of me.

E-25 Question: The Church history and practices are confusing to me. Is there a better way to better understand what my Church is about?

Answer: Sure – try to find ways to get a little better informed. Find time for bible study, consult the Catechism of the Catholic Church, join spirit-building groups at the parish, go to some conferences, attend a retreat, make an appointment with a priest for an office consultation, join the parish RCIA, either as a seeker or as a sponsor. These are just a few of your resource possibilities.

That said, one of my little tricks is to go back to the very basics. WWJD is not just a logo on a T-shirt. ***What would Jesus do?*** How would he look at the question? Did he admit that he didn't come to save the just, but the unjust? Yes! Are we the sinners he wanted to be with, to pray for, to save and heal? Yes, we are! So, how would he answer your questions about church and faith? Imagine his answer – his smile – his welcome – his healing.

The other basic thing would be to review the Apostles and how they talked about their time with Jesus, and what did he instruct them to teach to the world? Read the Acts of the Apostles again – and the Gospels themselves. What did Peter, John, James, and, of course, Paul – what did they preach about? Did they believe that Mary was an extremely special selection of God? Yes! Did they believe in her perpetual virginity? Yes! Did the first letter of John and the epistle of James talk about how to remove sin from your and my life? Yes! Scripture always has answers for us TODAY, not just for those who heard the words 2,000 years ago. These are the basic resources that any Catholic should be using to shape their own spirituality.

E-26 Question: Did I hear that Pope Francis has excommunicated the Mafia?

Answer: Yes, he certainly did. While in Calabria, Sicily, a Mafia stronghold, on June 21st 2014, he stated, "Those who follow the path of evil, like the Mafiosi do, are not in communion with God; they are excommunicated. When one does not adore the Lord God, one becomes an adorer of evil, like those who live lives of crime and violence. Your land, which is so beautiful, knows the signs and consequences of this sin. This is what the 'Ndrangheta (n.b. : an ultra-vicious crime syndicate based in Calabria) is: the adoration of evil and contempt for the common good."

Whew, what a wonderful stance to finally take. Though the Mafiosi have always considered themselves solidly Catholic, Catholicism no longer considers them worthy of the term. Excommunication, of course, is subject to review and reconsideration under the right circumstances, but it seems unlikely to occur.

Pope Francis has been a wonderful example to the world of how a true Christian lives his life and embraces the needs of others. We are blessed to have his common sense and loud voice leading so well from the Vatican.

Please, dear Lord, let your new Vicar continue to show the world that Christianity has a heart and a voice.

E-28 Question: What might distinguish a Catholic who is mature in faith and spirituality?

Answer: Big question, and I'm sure I can't answer it definitively. However, the further we are on our journey home, we might find the following characteristics to show up in a God fearing personality:

> The ability to realize that all judgment can be deferred to God. That our perception of other people is not what God sees, and we can see them and their actions in the light of compassion and love – let the judgment go.

> The ability to forgive those who damage us in some way. That only means we take the resentment, the hate and the desire for revenge off of our own shoulders. It does not mean we have to forget lessons learned from the encounter or try embracing others in a love that they don't welcome or reciprocate.

> That we learn to be inclusive in those we accept into our lives – the old and the young, the ugly and the beautiful, the wise and the

less so, the straight and the gay, the prayerful and the godless, etc. Even us bald guys need love! (especially us!!)

That we spend time in developing our relationship with God – through prayer and a daily awareness of His nearness and His love.

That we eagerly seek opportunities to share our faith with others, and do so with compassion and understanding.

That we treat each other with consideration and compassion and a determination to understand that we all have strengths and weaknesses, good and bad traits, tendencies to sin and tendencies to repent.

E-29 Question: Why do we see different colors of clothes on the priest at mass?

Answer: Well, you hit on the very intricate cycle of the Liturgical Year, also followed by many other major Christian faith expressions. First of all, our church New Year starts the last Sunday of November, with four weeks of Advent, a time of reflection on spiritual readiness, and of preparing to welcome the birth of Jesus. *The color of vestments is violet or purple,* reminding us to thoughtfully review our spiritual health.

In following the Proper of Seasons, or the Liturgical Year, the Christmas period comes next, lasting for two weeks from the evening of December 24th, through the feast of the Baptism of Jesus on January 9th. *The color of vestments is white or gold*, in celebration.

Ordinary Time follows. This doesn't mean "usual" or "not special", just that the Latin word *ordinal* means *"numbered",* and these weeks each carry an identifying number. There are either 33 or 34 weeks of ordinary time throughout the year – a few between Christmas and Lent, and bunches of them from Pentecost to the end of the year on the last Sunday of November, the feast of Christ the King. *Vestment colors are green*, honoring the growth of the church and our own spiritual maturing.

Lent starts with Ash Wednesday, when we receive a mark crossed onto our foreheads, and either a reminder that we ourselves are destined to eventually return to ashes, or an admonition to follow the Gospels and to sin no more. Lent lasts six weeks, and is intended to be intensely reflective and to encourage repentance. We are asked to be a little sacrificial during meatless Fridays and through fasting. We should remind ourselves of Christ's own sacrifice, and how it offers us salvation if we keep ourselves prepared. *Vestments are purple*, a sign of sorrow for sins, and of penance.

The shortest church season starts with Holy Thursday, through until Easter Vigil. (three days) This is called the Passiontide or Triduum during which we follow Jesus sorrowfully from the Last Supper, through His death on the Cross, and to His isolation in the tomb.

Then comes the triumph of Christ's rising from the dead on Easter morning. Easter season lasts for 50 days, until Pentecost, which honors the gifts of hope, strength and wisdom given freely to the Apostles and disciples by the Holy Spirit. *Easter season's vestments are again white or gold*, in celebration.

Then, until the end of the Liturgical Year, ordinary time prevails, reverting to *green vestments*.

Exceptions: *Red vestments are worn on all feast days of martyrs and the Apostles, signifying blood shed for faith. Also red is worn on Palm Sunday and Good Friday.

*White and gold can be worn on any major feast day, or on celebrations such as Baptisms or weddings. We also use white for funerals, in celebration of the life and eventual resurrection of the deceased. (Purple or black vestments are also authorized for funerals, but seldom are used for that purpose anymore.)

*Rose or pink may be worn on the third Sunday of Advent and the fourth Sunday of Lent.

*White vestments with blue trim may be worn on feasts honoring the Blessed Virgin.

E-30 Question: The term Vatican 2 keeps coming up in Catholic talk. What is that, and why is it so important?

Answer: Vatican 2 refers to the 21st General Council of the Church, in which all bishops of the world were called together to decide questions that affected the way the Church runs. Commonly called The Second Vatican Council, this took place 50 years ago, from 1963 through 1965. In Church time, that is still fairly recent. This, then, is the second time a general council has been called which has been sited within the Vatican. The previous was in 1870.

Each of the 20 councils that had been held between the year 325 AD and today had been called to combat heresy, apostasy, or to excommunicate or punish, as well as to establish the truth of Church doctrine. Vatican II, however, was called to help Catholicism repair brokenness within Christian faith expressions; to welcome reconciliations, to seek common grounds of faith, and to modernize the ways in which we celebrate our existence.

The decision to bring Catholic practices into a modern, technologically oriented era was that of Pope John XXIII, who proclaimed his intent on Oct. 11, 1959, stating that he intended to "open a window to the world." The actual council was declared open on Oct. 11, 1962, bringing some 260 bishops together from around the world. It also seated and included many other faith expressions in deliberations, so that prevalent views and decisions could better reflect a wider view of God's church.

Pope John XXIII died on June 2, 1963, while the council was still in full session, and was promptly replaced with Pope John VI, elected on June 21, 1963.

The Second Vatican Council was declared closed on December 8, 1965, the feast of the Immaculate Conception.

The changes brought about through Vatican II had great impact, and their implementation is considered a pivotal point in the existence of Catholicism. Most defined a willingness to engage other Christian faith expressions in discussions designed to mend differences of viewpoints and dogma. Another aspect was to simplify Catholic practices and liturgies so that congregations could better participate fully and knowledgeably. Mass was allowed to be said in any vernacular language, provided the prayers were accurate translations of the previous Latin ones. Altars were to face the congregation, and altar rails were to be taken down if possible. Vestments were simplified, doing away with the rampant ceremonialism that had crept in over the centuries.

These changes, along with many others designed only to return the Church to a more simplistic era of history, did not go unchallenged by elements within and without the Church structure. No dogma was changed. No fundamental beliefs were changed. Scripture study was vastly expanded. The rank of Deacon was returned to the clerical structure. The Rite of Christian Initiation for Adults was reinstated as a route to conversions, much as it had been used at the dawn of the Church. The Eucharistic fast was reduced to one hour before reception. Diocesan tribunals were reminded to be compassionate in decisions made regarding the dissolution of marriage through annulments.

Vatican II is now over 50 years old, and is still gradually becoming implemented on a global scale, sometimes well beyond what had been envisioned or even desired by the Council itself. It remains very controversial among conservative Catholics, and has proven to be of great promise in ending centuries of Church lethargy and "inbreeding".

We pray, O Lord, that the deliberations of the Second Vatican

Council will bring a renewal of faith and hope to a staggering and tired church.

E – 30 QUESTON: Why does God cause or permit suffering? Is He not a compassionate being?

ANSWER: Yes, of course He is all-loving and all-compassionate. However, our world has been left flawed and in darkness since our first man and woman denied Him through sin. We are left with a human nature which is fragile, and has a definite, though unknowable, span. We are born in pain, are given free will to decide how we will live, develop, learn, grow and become people of worth – or not. I don't think God ever causes pain or suffering, and grieves with us when it happens. The natural world in which we exist is full of dangers and disasters, with which we must learn to cope or die. We are challenged to become faith filled followers who obey the commandments He has given us. Pain and loss, anger, sorrow and violence are offset by triumph, love, excitement, joy and compassion. By being open to all of these in our lives we develop into mature people, hopefully embracing a choice to be members of God's family, then are able to move on to a perfect afterlife.

It is difficult here, my God, and sometimes so hard to live with the loss of loved ones, the existence of pain, suffering, war, pestilence and natural disasters. The perfection of your world beckons us ever onward, and the hope you have given us is like a shining star to our tired eyes.

E – 31 QUESTION: There is a word in the Lord's Prayer that confuses me. "do not **LEAD** us into temptation" Does God really lead us into sin?

ANSWER: That question comes up pretty often, since obviously God does not, and cannot, cause us to sin – and certainly isn't going to ***lead*** us into committing it. No, the original translation from Greek into English was a bit off the mark, and might have been better stated as, "do not allow us to enter into temptation." There – a whole different perspective!

My continual tendency to fall into the embrace of a sinful life must be a great source of sorrow, my dearest Jesus. Continue to hold my hand, to counsel and guide and beckon, that I may come to know you here and in the afterlife.

E-32 QUESTION: Was there an actual Adam and Eve, or is that simply folklore?

ANSWER: I don't know – I wasn't there. But, no – to answer your question, there needs only to be a belief that there was an origin to our version of humanity, and that we, the family of God, are all descended from His creation. The very words Adam and Eve simply mean first man and first woman. So yes – they certainly existed at the very root of our family tree, and did indeed disobey God's instruction, becoming the first human sinners. This caused us to no longer be born into perfection, but to need to earn our salvation through struggle. This disobedience is sometimes called Original Sin, though I think it exists only as a lack of God's light, not a tangible black mark on our souls.

We are created to be perfect people, my God, carved and shaped into your own likeness. We sorrow at our loss of grace, but are so comforted by the ways in which you continue to hold us in your loving arms.

E – 32 QUESTION: Can all sin be forgiven?

ANSWER: Yes, of course. Whatever we do can be forgiven, regardless of how big the disobedience … sin … has been. God's mercy is endless, and the forgiveness won by the sacrifice on the cross is also without limit. Our sincere contrition is required, as is an honest desire to prevent the sin from reoccurring.

There are two types of contrition. The first is sorrow for sin because that sin has hurt God, who is all good, and worthy of every bit of obedience we can give, simply because He is worthy of our endless adoration. That is "perfect" contrition.

The second is being sorry for having committed sin, but only out of fear of having brought about God's anger and retribution. Fear of a loss of salvation. Fear of an eternity in Hell. That is "imperfect" contrition.

Minor sins, ones we used to call "venial" can be forgiven by reception of the sacraments and quiet promises to God to avoid the occasion of sins in the future.

Those offenses we used to title "mortal" are, of course still very serious, and require they be confessed during reception of the Sacrament of Reconciliation.

Our offenses are grave, my God, and they occur with great repetition. Yet in your compassion and love, they can be forgiven if we approach your throne as repentant sinners – as heirs to the salvatory death of Jesus crucified.

E – 33 QUESTION: Ex 20:4-5 says we cannot worship idols. Aren't the statues in churches simply that?

ANSWER: That passage reads; "*You shall not make for yourself an idol or a likeness of anything in the heavens above or on the earth below or in the waters beneath the earth;*

You shall not bow down before them or serve them. For I, the Lord, your God, am a jealous God ..."

This has always been an apparent instruction not to worship anything other than the one true God – not to bow down to man-made idols instead of giving homage to the creator of everything. It was a common practice in superstitious times to make up divinities and to worship those images as gods. That is obviously wrong!

On the other hand, is it sinful to have a picture of your parent in a wallet, or of a loved spouse in a bedside frame? Is it wrong for a budding young baseball player to have cards of his favorite players in his room? Of course not, because the purpose of those things is not to worship, but to be remind us of things or people we cherish. In the same way, statues in church are not worshiped, but are simply used to remind us of the spiritual excellence of lives lived well, and to try to learn how to best emulate their success as followers of God. If we bow before them, it is only a reverence for the God which they followed, and if we expect anything of the saints those statues represent, it would only be that they join us in prayer and worship to the one, the triune Godhead, creator of all things.

Thank you, God, for those who have loved me, and for whom I still bear great love. Let me never forget their faces, or what they have meant to me. May you welcome them into your kingdom, and may they continue to pray for my strength of faith and observance of your laws.

E – 34 QUESTION: I've been away from my Catholic faith for quite a while, but I'd love to return and gain back the reverential feelings I used to have. Do you have any suggestions for me?

ANSWER: Yes, of course – and, welcome home! You may want to talk to a priest, and probably to receive a valid confession in the Sacrament of Reconciliation. That done, meet some members of the congregation, and make new friends. Eventually you'll probably want to weave your life back into the church by joining groups, whether bible studies, men's or women's

clubs, etc. If you'd like a recommendation for some excellent books, seek answers from someone you admire and trust. But, you can't go wrong reading some of Matthew Kelly's books, such as *Rediscover Catholicism* or *The Four Signs of a Dynamic Catholic*, and others. Scott Hann has a nice conversion story called *Rome Sweet Home* – and of course – there are thousands of others. Some parishes even have a ministry which will help you get comfortable "back in the pews".

Welcome home, you who have wandered to the farthest shores of your spirit.

E – 35 QUESTION: What does it mean to be "born again"?

ANSWER: Most non-Catholic religions use the term to mean having a spiritual awakening, an infusion of the energy of the Holy Spirit. Catholics, of course, have probably already become members of God's family through Baptism, have been reinforced in faith through Confirmation, have received the Body and Blood of Christ through the Eucharist, etc. Still, there is something to be said for turning a corner in faith, becoming passionate and energetic in belief and in evangelization. All of us seek a wondrous relationship with God, and there is nothing wrong with achieving it. If asked, a Catholic should say, "Yes, I am born again in Christ. Yes, I have been anointed by the Holy Spirit and become a child of God. Isn't it grand!"

May my spirit ever experience the glorious joy of your presence, my adored one, my God and my all!

E-36 QUESTION: The priestly scandal has really discouraged me about Catholicism. Do you think that the celibate life causes such dysfunction?

ANSWER: No, absolutely not. You will find that virtually every pedophile is married, yet marriage does not cause pedophilia, any more than does celibacy. There simply are people who prey on others, especially on the young and weak. It usually takes on a sexual connotation, and can be caused by insecurities, mental disturbances, thwarted sexuality or simple misuse of authority. Regardless, it is a horrendous and twisted betrayal of trust. There is evidently a certain percentage of society as a whole prone to become pedophiles, but luckily it is a very small percentage. In the Catholic church it has seemed to be about only 1% of priests who have betrayed their calling, though it is contrary to all that is good. That leaves 99% who are wonderfully committed to the good of their flocks – period.

We have seen for years the sexual failings of many public pastors of many different faiths, including those whose chosen medium is television. These perversions must be stopped, brought into the light, and prevented from ever occurring again. That has been the worst failing of Catholic leadership – to try and cover up such egregious actions, and that mindset no longer exists among Catholic bishops.

Give comfort to your great servants, my God, the leaders of your flock who have been ever faithful to you in their work and worship.

E – 37 QUESTION: Can atheists or agnostics find salvation? After all they reject or refuse to believe in the very existence of God!

ANSWER: First, understand that not all atheists or agnostics have had sufficient opportunity to come to know of God in sufficient detail to make a reasoned decision to either reject or embrace. God's family includes all people of "good will" – those who live in accord with His principles, with high moral standards, good ethics, and compassionate actions – regardless of where they are. It is said, with a great deal of unfortunate truth, that there are no atheists in foxholes under fire.

Regardless, it is not up to us to decide for God who He will or can accept into Heaven, nor can we speak with His voice or authority, though there are certainly those who try. Believe in the good that resides in people. Believe that God dwells in each member of his creation, and that each member of that family has the ability to live in honor and truth.

There is reason, though, to feel that those who have heard God's word, and who have come to believe Jesus was also that Word made flesh, have then a much better basis for understanding how to live in accord with that word. Of course, those who have received a thorough familiarization with Jesus,

Christianity, with the concepts of God, the Holy Spirit, and the need for living with compassion and love – and who have then rejected and turned away from those beliefs, undoubtedly have much to fear of God's wrath in return.

Remind me when I falter in faith, my Jesus, that your sacrifice was made for me, and for all mankind. I need to know that I can somehow become worthy of your pain and suffering on my behalf. I love you with an undying passion!

E – 38 QUESTION Is all of God's truth contained in the Bible?

ANSWER: No, not necessarily. The Holy Scriptures undoubtedly contain God's teachings for our lives, and are a wondrous resource for faith. They are taken on faith as truly inspired, and vital to our spiritual development.

Still, God's word comes gift packed to us at birth, in the form of a conscience which guides us as to right and wrong.

God's word comes to us through observing the actions of good people, who behave in concert with His commandments.

God's word comes to us very quietly, at times of meditation or in answer to prayer.

God's word certainly exists in the limitless resource we call Holy Tradition – all the scholarship, the additional spiritual texts, the endless testimony of holy men and women – and in the Magisterium – the teaching authority of mother church.

So, no – *Sola Scriptura* (*only through Scripture*) a common belief in non-Catholic faith expressions, is a very misleading concept.

There is such a great amount of knowledge in the world, Lord, much of it leading away from your love. Help me to rather embrace that knowledge that brings me toward my spiritual home, and eventually to my eternal home.

CHAPTER F – MARRIAGE AND FAMILY

F-1 Question: I know the Church prohibits abortion and contraception, but how does it feel about ways of increasing families, such as in-vitro fertilization, etc.?

Answer: Well, first of all, the Church only condones what it feels God has instructed… so the rules come from another source than just the Church. However, the feeling is that marriages are supposed to be a place of joy, wherein your love and intimacy results in children to nourish, protect and raise as spiritual beings. If you have difficulty producing children, certainly some methods that help the possibility of conception are acceptable – but not all. Of course adoption and "natural family planning" can be used. However, in-vitro fertilization (test-tube babies), and all its permutations, is outside the natural order of marital relations, therefore non-permissible, as is surrogate motherhood. All conception must occur as a result of natural marital coitus. Physical or hormonal dysfunctions that prevent pregnancy may be treated appropriately (surgically or chemically), though with dignity and loving interaction.

Have a fireside chat with a priest for deeper insights into these

subjects.

My Lord, help me to bring your precious gift of children into my life, that I may present them to Your loving embrace, and your holy Church.

F-2 QUESTION: I'm a conflicted Catholic! I believe in a baby's right to life, but have to admit that I also think that parents have the right to make abortion decisions without me interfering.

ANSWER: Your question requires a lengthy, detailed answer, but the short version ... the official position of the Catholic Church is that there is *no middle ground*. If you respect life... there is no other possibility other than to support the preservation of that life-regardless of circumstance!.

We lost our son a while back, and grieve at the loss. However, we unexpectedly ran across some pictures just a few days ago which detail a moving sequence of the birth, loving, feeding and cuddling of our wonderful granddaughter by our son and his wife, though they originally had to make a deliberate choice to continue the pregnancy.

What a gift those pictures are! What a gift is baby Jacqueline! Thankfully, the parents managed to get past money worries to decide on parenthood. Life is so precious, and every mother who decides to abort her fetus comes to know great loss and guilt later. How tragic for her! There are many options for placing unwanted children, and many families begging to be allowed to adopt! Can we let peer pressure, inconvenience, or economics cause another innocent death? It is a known fact that eventually the knowledge that they have destroyed a precious one often leads women who have aborted life to a great depression and terrible sense of sadness and guilt. Please, please remember that many women admit that if even one supporting person had argued for their baby's life, they would have carried the baby to term. As a Catholic and as a Christian, you are certainly called to be that one voice!

"God, we've prayed for great leaders, prophets, wise men, scientists to help us overcome scourges like plague and cancer – why haven't you answered our prayers?"

And God replies, "Oh, I answered your prayers all right. I've sent you all those people and more, but you keep aborting each of them."

F-3 Question: Just what is a Catholic annulment, and how is it different from a divorce.

Answer: A divorce is a term for a legal separation of married people according to civil law. It principally settles the distribution of assets, parental privileges and legal restrictions. The Church recognizes divorce, though it really dislikes bringing either divorce or separation into the existence of a sacramental marriage. Neither divorce nor separation actually releases people from a valid marriage according to Church law, as it is a contract made with God Himself, with priest and parish as simple witnesses. Being divorced, without remarriage, does not in any way diminish your rights as a Catholic.

The Church recognizes there are situations that cannot be permitted to continue in a marriage, however, including the abuse of spouse or children, and so allows for an existence apart of the married couple, a legal separation.

An annulment, however, actually dissolves the bonds of matrimony, but only under extreme and unusual circumstances. What must be proven before a court of canon law is that some flaw existed prior to the marriage ceremony. Extreme youth or immaturity. Forced marriage due to pregnancy or a father's shotgun. Keeping important facts secret, such as sexual dysfunction or capacity. Lying to the future spouse about wanting children, or the intent to use contraceptives without the other's knowledge. Having an undisclosed history of violence, insanity, disease, etc. An undisclosed previous marriage, still in existence or not. Several other pre-existing conditions may weaken the basic foundation of a marriage, and thus have a potential for invalidating it.

Thus an annulment (wiping away) says that the marriage was never a properly executed contract in the first place, and can thus be set aside. The children of such a marriage are considered fully legitimate, however.

Another type of annulment is called "Defect of Form", in which the proper form of a sacramental marriage between a Catholic and a non-Catholic or even two Catholics was not carried out in the first place. If the Catholic party knew that the Church could not recognize the existence of a civil marriage carried out before a non-religious entity such as a judge, justice of the peace or a wedding chapel run by a would-be Elvis impersonator – then the marriage can be set aside as non-sacramental. This sometimes can be a much simpler, faster form of annulment.

Most parishes have an "advocate" among the staff or clergy, who is to be of assistance in organizing a case for annulment by seekers. They sometime appear on their behalf before a diocesan tribunal, track paperwork, etc.

Catholics whose spouse is still alive may only remarry if the previous marriage has been set aside as non-existent through the annulment process, which can be lengthy, complicated and difficult to pursue.

Thank you, my God, for the joy I have found in my loving spouse, for her support and comfort, for her counsel and strength, for she fulfills my every need.

F-4 Question: Is it lawful according to the Church to use Viagra within a marriage if necessary?

Answer: There is nothing harmful about using some substance to make a marital partnership possible and productive in the face of an otherwise male erectile dysfunction. That, however, is the only situation where it is legitimate and allowed. Using it as some sort of recreational drug – not so much.

F-5 Question: I've heard that stem cell research is not allowed by the Church because it uses cells drawn from aborted fetuses. Is that right?

Answer: No, it's not. Actually, the stem cells drawn from fetuses are not suited for use anyway, as they seem impossible to control. When studies have been done, those cells have virtually gone berserk, causing severe damage.

Stem cells can be taken from adult subjects in several approved ways, and these seem to produce more potential uses – to fight cancer, rheumatoid arthritis, Parkinsons, and many other diseases. They may even regenerate major organs damaged by disease or trauma. Regardless of what you may have heard, stem cells need never come from aborted babies, and if they are not, they are acceptable both for research and eventual use.

Lord, you who see our struggles to live know that often our minds are on worldly things. Help us to live more in your certain knowledge and wealth of blessings, that our spirits may be nourished. If it be your will that we continue to explore alternate methods of health, assist us in our research, but do not let us become perverted by the false promises of Satan while we do so.

F-6 Question: Are Catholics allowed to marry non-Catholics?

Answer: Yes, of course they are, but there are conditions imposed by the Church.

First of all, neither may have been divorced, unless the former spouses have become deceased, or if the previous marriages have been declared void by a decree of nullity.

Secondly, both partners must participate in the usual pre-Canna marriage preparation classes, which help prepare both parties for the stresses of marriage:

Thirdly, the non-Catholic party must agree not to prevent the Catholic spouse from practicing their faith, nor use contraceptives, or prevent future children from being baptized or being raised in the Catholic faith.

Fourth, if such a marriage has any potential of creating scandal, it may still go forward, but without a large public participation in the ceremony.

Bless our joining, O Lord, that our family may grow in love and good health, and teach us how to lead each other and our offspring to follow in your footsteps.

F-7 Question: Is artificial birth control possible under certain circumstances?

Answer: No, I'm afraid not, if you are talking about mechanical interventions such as condoms, IUD devices or chemical substances such as "the pill" or the "morning-after pill". Anything which produces an aborted fetus, or surgeries that result in the same are forbidden. *Coitus interruptus* or alternate types of penetration are also unacceptable.

The only recognized forms of preventing natural pregnancies are:

First: Not having intercourse at all, by mutual consent only, which unfortunately circumvents the prime purpose of marriage.

Second: By using natural family planning, in which intercourse is attempted only during periods of reduced fertility – again only by mutual consent and understanding.

Some thought has been given to the use of methods which do not kill or reject an active fetus, but simply interfere with conception before it occurs. However, the Church maintains that there is not a significant difference as each circumvents the purpose of marriage, and the ban must be observed.

It should be noted that the creation of children is considered by the Church to be the entire reason for marriage, and that protecting such offspring and providing a nurturing love and caring within the family – these are the sacred duties of parents.

Our struggle in the world as parents, workers, caregivers, homeowners and lovers leaves us very little time to think of you, Lord. Help us through your endless blessings to keep our focus on the importance of faith and spirituality, that our marriage show you our adoration and commitment to each other in your name.

CHAPTER G - MORALITY

G-1 QUESTION: I keep hearing that pride is wrong – that we must become humble to be good Christians. Is that right?

ANSWER: Proverbs 29:23 is one of the hundreds of places in the bible that says in essence "*the proud shall be brought low, and the humble shall prosper.*" (There is a great deal of difference in some of the biblical translations of that phrase.) What they don't say is that a more accurate translation to English of the Greek word for pride might be "*arrogance*" or "*false pride*" instead of simply "*proud*". I certainly hope you and I have lots of pride in our honest accomplishments, our babies, our capabilities, our faith, and in so many other things. God didn't make junk, and has blessed us all with special talents, and led us through the difficulties that strengthened us and taught us compassion and true humility. Unless we recognize our intrinsic worth we'll never strain to reach our potential. If we have a poor self-image, it's not humility – it's only depression! Justified pride includes a humble realization that we have been gifted by God in order to accomplish great things. What a blessing! When our attitude becomes arrogance, though, we start to fail God's law. What Christ never wants to find in our hearts is false pride, arrogance, self-importance or self-centeredness. Love of, compassion for and service to others rises from a knowledge of self, our capabilities and our talents. None of us needs or wants to become like the Pharisees of the bible who "*widened their phylacteries and lengthened their tassels, prayed loudly in public and thought themselves better than other men*". Jesus didn't like them very much!

Lord, lead me to a knowledge of your gifts, that I may share your blessings with those I meet. I give you all that I am. Please direct and use me so that I might fulfill the purpose for which you have created me.

G-2 QUESTION: Would you think it appropriate for a gay man to apply to a seminary seeking a life as a priest?

ANSWER: Sure, why not? In former years it was quite common for that to occur, but I'm afraid these days the rector's admission panel would try to screen out such a personality. There is a mistaken belief that a homosexual has more of a tendency to be a pedophile than a heterosexual, but that perversion exists outside of either sexual predilection. If someone is being called by God to be His sanctified priest, there must be a willingness to be chaste, especially after taking the vows at ordination. If an applicant for the priesthood is willing to be celibate, non-practicing in sexuality, it doesn't matter what his preference might otherwise be. Again, remember that pedophilia is a mental disturbance resulting from an immature sexuality, a desire to exert control over the helpless, or some other determining factor than homo or hetero-sexuality.

G-3 Question: I keep hearing that the Da Vinci Code book/movie is anti-Catholic and anti-Christian. Is that true?

Answer: Well… I remember back in my younger years there were weekly pulpit announcements by the pastor denouncing some movie or other. I recall the name Bridgett Bardot coming up once in a while. Public depictions of nudity and even shared beds were deeply frowned on, and understandably so. Still, I think the Church wisely backed away from trying to mandate viewpoints on politics and entertainment, though heaven knows we could always use good moral guidance. There are still many Catholic sites on the internet, etc. where such moral reviews of media and public policy are still provided.

As for my personal view of The Da Vinci Code, I think it can present some confusing issues for anyone not grounded in Christian history. I have to admit, I enjoyed the book as an exciting, fast-paced piece of fiction, but the author's claims of accurate research have been under fire by respected scholars. My suggestion would be to steer clear of the movie unless you can keep your perspective that it is simply fiction. While engrossing, it is at best written from a highly biased viewpoint. Be sure the many outlandish claims such as Jesus being married to Mary Magdalene, etc. can be taken with a really big grain of salt. It's probably a good idea to understand there is definitely anti-Christian bias in the movie, and to decide not to make the studios any richer with our hard-earned money.

Stick to the basic Catholic beliefs that guide families on issues of faith and morals, and – if you want some wild and entertaining fiction, I've always been partial to Bugs Bunny myself. "Eh, what's up, Doc?"

Lord, what I see with my eyes has power to harm me. What I perceive with my mind can do the same. But what I see with a purity of heart and a heartfelt love for you can never bring me into conflict with your desire for me.

G-4 Question: What the heck is wrong with our young people these days?

Answer: I talked this over with a friend who is a priest. His answer is that our young people are *wonderful*, but if we're not satisfied with their behavior sometimes… who do we look to? Why – those who formed their little characters, of course – the parents!

Do you realize that Europeans don't separate adult television programming from family fare? Why not? They can do it because they know the children will be watching as part of a family – not alone and unattended. It's expected the parents, grandparents, and other members of the household supervise their activities, and the things they watch. Do we? The world has sure changed for us balding boomer-types! Movies, television, computers, the Web, synthetic drugs, cell phones, latch-key children, one-generation households, affluence won by slavish dedication to careers…. these things don't permit us to even begin to know the *who, what, why* and *how often* things about our own kids. Children haven't changed, but they certainly are living in different situations – more threatening isolation – than we used to. They need our guidance, not our friendship and our permissiveness. They need hugs, lots of them. They need affirmation – to be shown our pride in their accomplishments, and our commiseration when they fail after making a good effort. They need our love and our values. They need our experience and knowledge. They don't need to be ignored. One great place to start is with Christian example and guidance. All the good parts of character – ethics, morals, appreciation for others, honesty, integrity.... whatever!,... easily trace back to values instilled by God-fearing parents, living their religion more than one hour a week. If we expect teachers and preachers to raise them for us, we'd better re-evaluate!

I love being a member of your family, my Lord God, yet remind me always that I owe so much to the family that bore and raised me, and so much also to the family with which you have blessed my marriage. Thank you!

G-5 Question: What is sin, really?

Answer: That's a pretty easy question to answer. Basically, any thought, deed or action which a person knows is contrary to God's will, and yet is willingly and deliberately engaged in. There is no sin if there is no realization of wrong-doing, and there is no sin if someone is coerced, tricked or forced into carrying out the action.

For a nice overview of how to live a sin-free existence in close accord with God's wishes, read again the 1st letter of John and the letter of James.

Let me always seek guidance for my life from your sacred scripture, O God.

G-6 Question: What is the worst sin?

Answer: Whichever might condemn you to a loss of the eternal beatific vision, of course. These sins would be what we used to call "mortal" or "deadly" sins, meaning they could cause the loss of Heaven, a loss of God's grace and company. Now we recognize that there is always an insult to God in any sin, though some are, of course, worse than others.

One of the most serious, and often overlooked is the sin of scandal. This is any action that causes other people to become diminished in faith, or to be swayed away from a life of goodness and belief by witnessing how we live our own lives.

According to the bible, (Mk 3:29), the only unforgivable sin is blasphemy against the Holy Spirit, in which a person denies completely the existence and/or the authority of God, or defames the goodness of the God's Holy Spirit.

Since God is love, anything that damages others, or even the integrity, dignity and spirituality of your own person – God's temple - can be considered sinful. Hate, bullying, physical damage, murder, disobedience of the Commandments – there is an endless possibility of sin, and we can always use the conscience He gave us to judge the rightness or wrongness of our action. God, however, is not like Santa Claus, with a list of good or bad boys and girls, but watches in sorrow when His rules are disobeyed. He also offers endless forgiveness for those who honestly seek it.

Dear Lord, I know your arms encircle me with love, even when I stray from the path of goodness. Walk with me a while, as I journey, that I may have your pleasant company, your advice, your wisdom and your forgiveness for the ways in which I have failed you.

G-7 Question: I find myself using terrible language or cursing sometimes. Is this a serious thing or not?

Answer: Well, most of the things we spout aren't really curses at all – simply language in extremely poor taste. An actual curse asks that God harm another person, or even send them to Hell. Yes – that's bad! Disrespecting God in any way or taking His name in vain is extremely bad! But even if we use just rude gestures or language in our dealings with others, it can be dangerous, damaging, and lessens us. When our language causes somebody else distress, conveys insult, ridicules, demeans or ignores the rules of civilized behavior – we truly cause real harm, often more than we might realize. If nothing else, we are always called to be great examples of Christian values, and soft words do that a little better than *@!!!#%*!

I know my lips are called to be pure, my Lord. That my words be gentle and compassionate. Remind me at times of stress, so that my actions reflect only your goodness and welcome.

CHAPTER H - HOLY SCRIPTURE

H-1 Question: (The bible passage from Matthew 24:32-35 seems to predict that heaven will pass away. Can you explain this?

Answer: These wonderfully prophetic passages predict the fall of the Temple (accomplished about 38 years later) but Jesus' words also speak of the end times, in which there will be turmoil and suffering. (see also Mark 13) He warns against following false prophets, and advises that the world will eventually polarize into segments of good versus evil. The phrase (Mt 24:35) "*Heaven and Earth will pass away, but my words will not pass away*" simply emphasizes by mild exaggeration the eternal significance and truth of His words. It certainly does not mean that Heaven will ever become extinct.

Your peace, O God, fills my heart, and my soul exalts in your presence.

H-2 Question: A few days ago, the daily gospel (see Mark 8:15) mentioned "the leaven of the Pharisees". What does that mean?

Answer: This is a warning from Jesus telling His followers to beware the influence of Pharisees, Sadducees and Herod – none of whom were worthy of trust. Leaven, (yeast) is a biological contaminant added to bread dough. As it breaks down the structure of the flour the resulting bubbles are trapped in the baking process, leaving "raised bread". Leaven also causes quick spoilage of the finished product, which is why un-leavened bread was always carried on a long journey. The bread brought by those leaving Egypt with Moses; the bread eaten during the Passover and the Last Supper; the sacred hosts – the consecrated Body of Christ we eat during the Eucharist is all unleavened, or pure, with no contamination of mold, mildew or yeast.

The people Jesus mentioned undermined the purity of the Hebrew faith. God's warning is for us to be very wary of the teaching and leadership of the "Pharisees", etc., in our lives, as they dilute and reject God's law, living a sinful, self-centered existence and providing terrible examples to those seeking faith. How about those whom we follow as leaders – are they "leavened" with corruption or pure, dedicated and fully trustworthy? Are we ourselves worthy examples of Christian faith, helping others to grace, or are we "leavening"?

If my influence is more disruptive, Lord, than inspiring, help me come to a better understanding of how best to be "Church" to others. Help me be "eucharist", to be your family on earth, and to encourage all others to join in your celebration here.

H-3 Question: I keep hearing the term "rapture" in sermons by other faiths. Can you explain what this means?

Answer: Well, " Rapture" involves having all believers miraculously lifted away from earth and taken to Heaven at the end of time, missing the hardships expected to plague the unbelievers "left behind". (This was the subject of a recent group of fiction books, the "Left Behind" series, later a TV movie.) The concept of "rapture" takes the words in Paul's letter to the Thessalonians somewhat out of context with the *rest* of the bible. *1 Th 4:16-17* predicts a great shout, the trumpet of God ringing out, and all the dead rising for judgment. Then (*verse 17*,) "*We who are alive and remain will be caught up together with them in the clouds to meet the Lord in the air, and so we shall always be with the Lord.*" In *2 Th*, we read about "one man being taken and one man left behind", etc. All of this has been built up by some faith expressions into a belief that if we only have faith in God, and are "saved, by accepting Jesus Christ as our personal Lord and Savior", we will rise to meet Him in glory, in the clouds, in the air before or during the Last Judgment.

"Rapture" seems to presume that believers are spiritually perfect, worthier than others, and possess inside knowledge. It generates a belief that every right-living Christian is automatically saved without judgment!

Jesus Himself said it is not for man to know or understand the last days, so the Catholic Church disowns the concept of Rapture. We are told that to pass judgment we have to stay free of sin, tuned-up spiritually, and ready for whatever our appointed hour brings! It's a firm church belief that each of us will undergo a particular judgment at the moment of death, and also a final judgment at the end of time. The concept of "rapture", though pleasant, expects to somehow slip past all that simply by believing in Jesus. It is based on some isolated biblical words, and on a concept called *(warning, warning Will Robinson – big word alert!)* dispensationalism. This practice allows a rearranging of the Bible in ways that can lead to "new" teachings – including the exclusionist idea that "good" people will be *raptured*, avoiding the turmoil expected during the Last Days.

To some extent, though, the official Catholic beliefs neither embrace nor deny the possibility of what some call The Rapture, but certainly tend to discourage followers from betting their eternal existence on the concept that all believers will automatically be saved.

May God fill each of us with blessings, strength and faith, especially in those final days, and grant us forgiveness and mercy, that we may find eternal salvation in His arms.

Lord, bring me into the rapture of your love, into a knowledge of your goodness, that I may worship you for eternity.

H-4 Question: My non-Catholic friend talks about Jesus having brothers and sisters! Is that true?

Answer: Well, I know where the idea came from, though it's basically off-track. Yes – Jesus has brothers and sisters, and …here we are!

But to answer your question on another level, the Bible mentions the "brothers" of Jesus several times (see Mt 1:25 and Mt 13:55, among others), and people have assumed, wrongly, that this meant Mary had other children besides our Lord.

These words are translated loosely from Hebrew and Aramaic, simplistic languages which do not have separate words for brother, sister, cousin, stepchild, house guest, in-laws, close friend, etc. For instance, we see that James and Joseph are called "brothers" in Mt 13 though we know very well these are sons of a different Mary, wife of Clopas.

Another possibility (though remote) is that St. Joseph, possibly being older than our Blessed Virgin, could have had previous children to bring into a second marriage.

This is one result of having only a bible from which to learn. Though it is a wonderful, God-inspired resource, … there are additional sources of information. The Apostles always taught that Mary remained a true virgin throughout her life, and that Jesus was an only child. The trouble is, when a religion breaks away from the church Jesus founded, they have to renounce the apostolic tradition and teaching authority of the Catholic Church. All three founders of the protestant movement, Martin Luther, Calvin and Zwingli – some 1500 years later, still embraced a firm belief in the eternal virginity of our Blessed Mother. Without using all three – Bible, tradition *(other valid and respected sources of historical Christian resources*), and magisterium (*the authority to teach given the Church through the Great Commissioning)* – you'll get an incomplete picture!

Have patience with my imperfection, my God! Help me to study your word with the guidance and understanding of the scholarship of your church. Help me to find the goodness in all those I meet, and the understanding to see that all who seek you do so with a happy heart.

H-6 Question: The number 40 keeps popping up throughout scripture. Noah – rained for 40 days and 40 nights; Moses – led the Israelites for 40 years; Jesus – fasted for 40 days in the desert, etc., etc. Does this have special meaning?

Answer: These questions really need more space to answer, but the quick version is that the number 40 was symbolically special throughout history, particularly to the people of Israel. This was not always a literal "40"– usually just meaning "a very large number" to a tribal people of little learning, but the number often also implied a period of hardship, struggle or punishment – to be followed by some sort of "rebirth". The Jewish people were historically one who used numbers in many symbolic ways, and you might note that the number 7 comes up very often in scripture, as it thought to represent perfection.

Jesus, may I find today in my heart a willing commitment to you that I did not possess yesterday, and may my tomorrows increasingly bring a purity and love to all that I am.

H-7 Question: The Baltimore Catechism told us we each have a guardian angel. Is this found in scripture?

Answer: There are several references in scripture, though each is difficult to interpret. (see Ps 34:7 and Mt 18:10). It has indeed been a belief of the Church throughout our history. The much newer *Catechism of the Catholic Church* firmly states (CCC 336) that each believer possesses an angelic companion. I do really believe that I have one, and that he/she says "*Oh no, REALLY? Not again!*" way too often!

I apologize to you, my angel, for the discouragement you must encounter in dealing with my weakness and sinfulness. May your influence and prayers never fail, and your intercession on my behalf continue in spite of my failings.

H-8 Question: I keep hearing that the end times are at hand. What do you think?

Answer: Well, the end times have been predicted every day for the last 2000 years, so I guess this year makes as good a guess as any. This is an instance where the word of God contained in the

Bible has been humanly interpreted in many different ways, some accurate, and some waaaay off base! Let the teaching authority of the Catholic Church help you understand bible predictions and spiritual expectations.

Basically, who cares when it happens? We believe in the second coming of Christ as an article of faith contained in the Creed we profess at mass. So, if we're doing our best to live within God's laws, let the trumpets sound!!! (If there are any doubts about being in good spiritual shape, though, it might be wise to go get dusted off a little.)

May we greet God every day as a full partner in our life journey; as our soul mate and friend.

H-9 QUESTION: Why aren't Catholics supposed to study the Bible?

ANSWER: Wow, that's a completely wrong idea, to start with! Catholics have always been encouraged to study sacred scripture and to meet and know God as He is present in His Word. Especially since the Second Vatican Council we've been urged to spend time with the Bible, asking in faith for guidance and inspiration. The problem can be that it's not easy to understand every nuance of scripture, and we are asked by the Church to seek its expertise when confusion reigns. Each book of the Bible contains exactly what God wants to teach us, but different authors used their own styles and words to convey God's message. Look for the intent within the words, be open to guidance from the Holy

Spirit, understand that the historical and cultural influences of thousands of years ago flavor the words, and know that many different styles of writing were used. Confusion can easily cause errors, especially when sections or words are taken out of context, or read too literally. We study the deeper meaning of scripture as a whole church, not as individuals. Enjoy the lessons the Bible brings us, but always be willing to accept the knowledge, the scholarship and the authority of the Church to help guide you toward, not away from, God's presence in the Bible. The Catholic Church came into being well before the New Testament writings, and can be counted to provide solid guidance in all things spiritual.

Help me, my God, find nourishment for my spirit and soul through your marvelous word.

H-10 Question: I've been wondering – who actually wrote the Bible?

Answer: Yes – me too! No, I'm not really being flippant, but we don't actually know the real human authors of much of the Bible. However, we take it as a major article of faith that God Himself deliberately inspired each and every word, meaning those words to be lessons to all generations. Now, we usually think of the Bible as a book, but in reality it's an assortment of 73 different stories, done by more than 40 different authors, in dozens of different formats. Some are literal history; some are exaggerated stories; some are deeply spiritual; some are law books; some are letters; some are even romances. Do we take the Bible literally? Of course! ... but in the sense that each part of the collection is exactly what God wanted to tell us, done in the style and words of the human author.

Still, the "author's" title on each book is often a bit fuzzy. Some books are obviously the work of several people, and many more have been compiled from spoken history, giving credit to someone well known for the authorship. Again, many books have been written by those who quote ideas and phrases "according to" some major prophet or apostle who came through teaching and preaching. Such a naming was considered a great and respectful honor

The Hebrew Testament comes to us intact from the Jewish people, and is the only bible that Jesus ever studied or read from. It contains 46 books. The first five form the Torah, and are thought by Jewish scholars to have been written or organized by Moses, and these books form the backbone of both the Hebrew and Muslim faiths.

The New Testament starts with the coming of the Messiah, Jesus. The first book of Gospels might be that of Mark, probably done 15 to 20 years after Jesus died. The entire New Testament was written by early Christians and was finished no later than the year 125, and probably quite a bit earlier. All current Christian faith expressions use the same 27 books of the New Testament as Catholics do, and most modern translations are produced by the joint efforts of researchers from many different faiths. The only real difference is that Catholic bibles contain 7 more books in the Old Testament than do protestant versions. We don't have space here to get into more detail, but know that Catholics wrote those 27 NT books, after sharing the stories orally for many years. They selected these volumes from hundreds of writings as truly inspired, and guarded with their lives the result for 15 centuries before anything like a "protestant" version came to be. It's time for all good Catholics to become very familiar with the Bible, but be sure to lean on the teachings of the Church for help in interpreting the meaning of the inspired, but sometimes confusing, messages.

(To answer a question from a person who wondered if Catholics were permitted to donate material or money to another religious charity – Jesus insists that we are each responsible to "feed the hungry, clothe the naked, shelter the homeless," etc., (the Corporal Works of Mercy) – and He sure didn't specify any boundaries. If it looks like the work being done is worthy – go for it!)

H-11 Question: Are all religious books or bibles acceptable to Catholics?

Answer: Well, that's a bit of a broad question. I suppose all truly religious books should bring us an expanded experience of faith, but there are definitely some which tout falsities and which could lead us astray. Be selective and careful! If you really need accuracy, be sure to search for the terms "imprimatur" and "nihil obstat" on the title pages of major religious works including bibles. These signify that Church officials have found nothing of objection therein.

Most bibles are the work of excellent scholarship, and usually the translations of modern versions have been accomplished in concert by historians of several faiths. There are indeed a few bibles which have been over-simplified (Readers Digest, etc.), some are written for the undeveloped minds of young children; most non-Catholic editions are written in the stilted court language of Elizabethan times (the 1500s AD) with thee, thou and such, which sound strange to those of us used to the New American Bible. Regardless, all of these can be used for study and exploration without harm.

There are a few editions which have been deliberately changed in small ways to challenge Catholic doctrine, so be aware that some few bibles need to be taken in that context.

Catholic bibles date from the first days of Christianity, staying unchanged for centuries. Catholic bibles also have 7 more books in the Hebrew (the Old) Testament, than do non-Catholic editions. The extra books are called deuterocanonical (*usable alongside those books which are canonical* – who makes up these words?!) All 27 books of the New Testament (which starts with the birth of the Messiah) are common to all Christian bibles, regardless of faith expression.

Your word is law, my God, and sweet upon my ears.

H – 12 QUESTION: Is the current Catholic Bible the only one we've ever used?

ANSWER: No, not at all. Once the canon of the Bible had been determined at the Council of Hippo in 393, the pontiff asked St. Jerome to come up with a complete compilation of these 73 books, translated from original texts into the then prevailing language of the Church – Latin. He completed the task, with the help of very few assistants, in 382 AD. This was known as the

Latin Vulgate edition, meaning it was written for common understanding and use. It was used up to 1752 AD after having finally been rendered the official bible of the Catholic Church at the Council of Trent in 1545. An English-language edition was eventually issued by scholars at the joint French cities of Douay and Rheims in 1752, and a later revision called the Challoner edition, *Douay-Rheims* became the accepted Church bible. This continued until 1985, when the one in general use today became the modern book of choice, known as the *New American Bible* (NAB). It has already been brought up to date by additional research – first of the New Testament, and just recently of the Old Testament. It is now called the *New American Bible Revised Edition* (NABRE). Either one is suitable for study and for proclaiming from the ambo at mass.

Protect the integrity of your Word as scripture, my God, that we may be guided through life and into life.

H – 13 QUESTION: Do we still have any of the original texts of scripture from the time of the Apostles?

ANSWER: No, we don't. Unfortunately the mediums used in writing were very fragile – mostly papyrus and vellum. These have long since turned to dust, but were faithfully copied by generation after generation of dedicated scribes and monks. We do, however, continually come across earlier and earlier source material that validates or even enhances our current knowledge of scripture.

We know that your Word is eternal and unchanging, my God, given to our benefit.

H – 14 QUESTION: Was the bible actually dictated by God?

ANSWER: No, God doesn't dictate. He does, however, inspire people to write in such a way as to teach what needs to be learned by his followers. The Canon of Scripture has been accepted as truly inspired writing by all the bishops of the world, meeting in general conclaves over many centuries. The authors themselves were permitted to couch these writings in any way with accomplished the objective, spoke truly to those who heard or read the words, and used terms and situational descriptions which brought comprehension of God's message. They are intended to be used by every generation of followers, and hold the entire teachings as inspired by God. The various books represent a broad spectrum of types, including prophetic, historic, love stories, songs, apocalyptic, and many other ways of getting the messages across.

Let me never be confused by the complexity of Scripture, O Lord, but to immerse myself in them so as to find a true guide toward everlasting grace.

H – 15 QUESTION: Why do I have to know scripture? Don't I just need to follow the teachings of the Church?

ANSWER: Well, you certainly do need to do that, but know that what the Church teaches comes from both 2000 years of sacred tradition **and** from the Holy Scriptures. If you don't have a working knowledge of both, you are not fully informed in faith, and tend to drift along in some degree of confusion.

There is also a term called *apologetics*, which is an ability to discuss knowledgably and reasonably the faith that Jesus left us. (1 Pt 3:15) *"Always be ready to give an explanation to anyone who asks you for a reason for your hope but do it with gentleness and reverence."* The very word "apology" now is used to mean a debasement of self, asking for forgiveness for having done something wrong. It originally meant, instead, being able to offer a reasoned argument for a belief. If you have no real grasp of God's word in the Scriptures, you cannot be the "everyday apostle" we are all called to be, when someone wants to question the basis for our faith.

Let me find your truths in my heart, my god, that your words may be on my tongue, reside in my brain and rule my innermost being.

H- 16 QUESTION: I think Martin Luther brought out a version of the Bible, didn't he?

ANSWER: Yes, he was the first to take advantage of the advent of the printing press, desiring to spread God's word to the common people. The "Luther Bible" as it came to be called, was radically rearranged, and several books were left out, or placed in what was called Apocrypha (not inspired, but usable for study and guidance). The language was, of course, German. It came out in 1522 (OT) and 1534 (NT). He translated from Hebrew, Greek and

Aramaic, with excellent scholarship, though he found fault with much of the original Christian canon.

Those who have gone before us were not always perfect people, my God. Let us then live so as to have finally brought honor from chaos, and a creation of hope to all who follow after.

H -17 QUESTION: What other bibles were brought out during the Reformation?

ANSWER: There were quite a few, but those in general circulation were the three versions issued at the behest of King Henry VIII after he split away from Catholicism to form the Church of England, the Anglican Church. These came out in the late 16th century, but were outdated by better informed translations ordered by King James. The *King James Bible*, the KJB, came out in 1604, containing all 73 canonized books, though these were later reduced to 66 by leaving out Tobit, 1 and 2 Maccabees, Judith, Baruch, Wisdom and Sirach.

The King James has been updated several times, and there is also an edition called the Revised Version. Each updating contains updated scholarship and accuracy of translation, and has been worked on by panels from many faiths. The King James Version is the origin of the "thees and thous" type of bible-speak, brought in only to honor the Elizabethan formal court language of the 1500/1600's, making it acceptable to the reigning monarch. Don't get too hung up in thinking that God only listens to us when we pray the way Queen Elizabeth liked to hear his words spoken.

Help us find truth in your Word, my god, regardless of where it is written or proclaimed. Help us find a way to reconcile with other divergent faiths that we may all find our way home to you.

CHAPTER I - DIVINE WORSHIP

I-1 Question: I had a couple of people knocking on the door, saying I was a poor Christian because I attend church on Sundays, instead of on Saturday as God's covenant with Moses demands. How should I have answered them?

Answer: Well, your new buddies need to take another look at covenant history themselves. Old Testament history demanded that the Lord's Day be kept holy, and considered that to be the 7th day of the week, or the Sabbath. However, Jesus said He came to fulfill a new covenant in our presence. All Christians, from the very beginning, have celebrated the 1st day of the week as the new Lord's Day, to honor Christ's resurrection from the dead. Early apostles, converts and disciples continued going to temple on Saturdays for many years, but would then meet again later (on Sunday, which starts at sundown on Saturday) as followers of Christ, reading from scripture, repeating stories of Jesus and His lessons, and consuming a blessed meal – a "Eucharist". By the year 70 AD, the followers of Jesus were barred from Jewish temples, and their Sunday celebrations evolved into what we know as the Mass. Sunday was firmly entrenched as the new

Sabbath for Christians. Regardless, it is still vital that we truly honor God on at least that one day of the week, trying to avoid worldly distractions, resting, attending Mass, receiving the Eucharist and praying.

I know, dearest Jesus, that I am called to be your apostle in this time, and in this life. Those who come to bring me to you are undoubtedly rich in Your love, so let me be compassionate and understanding when talking with them. Let the Holy Spirit bring me the words that will bring them to a fullness of life in You, or to simply allow them to continue worshiping You as they feel is right.

I-2 Question: I've occasionally attended Catholic masses. I've got to say our services seem more spirit-filled than yours!

Answer: There's might be some truth here, though outward appearances aren't everything. Unless you have an understanding of the Mass, with the real presence of Christ, Body and Blood, and the ancient majesty, symbolism and meaning of the celebration – it can look a little slow and confusing, especially to outsiders.

It got me to thinking though, – are we becoming people who just watch religion happening? Now, for those of us who have achieved a more .... well, *mature* age, we can remember that before Vatican II changed our conception of "church" in the early 1960's, we pretty much did just watch the priest say mass, consecrate the Eucharist, and listened as the choir and altar servers responded. But... the Vatican Council reminded us that WE are church – a family glorifying God by our unity and love. We participate in everything. "Church" meets in a building. "Church" happens on the Sabbath, and on every other day of the week. "Church" joins in! We are church by our beliefs; by our actions; by the way we raise our families; by the way we seek to help others in need; by the way we let ethics and Christian values guide our actions; by the way we contribute financially to the needs of our parish; by the way we live every part of our lives. Ancient Romans recognized Christians by the fact that "they love one another".

So look around at Mass – is our questioner right? Do we remember that each person we see has a spark of divinity inside? Is there reverence and prayer? Do we come in time to spend a few thoughtful moments on our knees before Mass starts? Is everyone joining the church family in joyful song, dressed to respect God's presence, receiving the Eucharist in awe and thanksgiving? Do we go home having "done" church, instead of taking the spirit home to share throughout the week? Baseball might be a great spectator sport, ….but religion?......sure shouldn't be!

The mass is the perfect liturgy for me, my God! You give me a chance to repent, a chance to forgive, a chance to belong, a chance to dine at Your table and to hear Your word proclaimed. Let my attention be focused, my mind remain open to Your influence, and my heart receptive to your love.

I-3 Question: Why does the priest combine water with the wine of consecration?

Answer: First of all, these "gifts" of wine and bread offered for consecration actually come from all of us – "*work of our hands*", etc. We "offer" them to God at the offertory of the mass. The water partially represents the "water" (the fluid surrounding the heart) that Jesus shed after death, mingled with blood, when pierced with a spear. (Jn 19:34) This truly proved His death, later conquered by a return to life following His stay in the tomb. It also somewhat represents that the water of our baptism leads us to Christ, who is present in the Holy Eucharist. Another purpose is that by combining us, (the water) to the sacred blood, we are joined completely with the saving blood of Christ. Much of Catholic liturgy uses symbolism to remind us of the basic beliefs and truths of our religion. By the way, the priest also places a small particle of the consecrated host into the main chalice of consecrated wine, thus symbolically rejoining the Body and Blood into the whole person of Christ.

There is another, more mundane reason for adding water to the wine. For centuries parishioners brought wine to mass for the priest to change at communion time into the sacred Eucharist. Sometimes that homemade vino was virtually undrinkable unless diluted a lot. Of course, regardless – consecration changed it into Precious Blood.

We receive from the blood that pours eternally from your side into our communion cups, my Jesus, and the blessings that flow with it are countless. Your gift to us is truly a treasure, and so increase my awareness, Lord, that I may use those blessings to attain an eternal reward.

I-4 QUESTION: What can I say when non-Catholic friends want to argue about religion?

ANSWER: Well, let's start with not losing those friends by arguing in the first place! Nothing says lovin' like something said from the heart… but without confrontation. If they can't talk without argument, then it's a subject you'll have to avoid, and simply let your faith and the way you live it speak for you. I guarantee they'll be watching.

Now, if you can have a productive, friendly conversation, great! They might want to know that we wrote the New Testament and guarded it for 1500+ years before it was changed by "newcomers". Let them know that all historians admit our faith was the only Christian church Jesus instituted, and that some humans – for reasons of their own – have chosen to split away from the tree. They will probably want to quote scripture passages, so get to know your stuff. Most newly minted Christian religions are "sola scriptura", using the Bible as their only source of God's word, and they can be pretty well informed. You might tell them that, besides the bible, we have a treasure trove of sources, academia, eyewitness accounts, and tons of other material that connect us to God's will. We call this "Tradition", and it's a valuable, vital and verifiable backbone to the Catholic faith. The other wonderful treasure we hold is called the "Magesterium", which is simply a word to describe Jesus' instruction to His apostles to "go forth and teach all nations", which gives the Catholic structure the right to instruct and guide its members. If some persons separate from this structure, where do they derive authority to interpret scripture or direct a flock away from the original? Remind them we have an unbroken succession of apostolic authority, physically and spiritually passed on for 2000 years.

If your bible knowledge isn't wonderful, start small, but start TODAY, to get better acquainted with it. Get a very good bible, preferably a Catholic edition with "*Imprimatur*" and "*Nihil Obstat*" on the publisher's page – but know that almost all major translations are excellent. Try to find a study edition with great footnotes to help you understand the meaning behind the words – God's messages to us are always there, but sometimes hard to dig out. (We read from the New American Bible in church, but the footnotes are a little sparse.) Know that the Catholic faith takes inspiration in context with the whole of the bible –never line by line "pullouts" that others might try to use to prove a point.

God bless and keep you safe in faith!

I-5 Question: Do all Catholics pray the same way around the world?

Answer: We are the only religion that is truly universal (which is what "catholic" actually means), so, yes – we all believe exactly the same things as outlined in the Creed we profess during mass. The language we use to praise God is always the one we're born into and comfortable with, and many local customs and traditions alter slightly the way our beliefs are expressed or celebrated. At each mass, everywhere in the world, the exact same readings can be heard during the Liturgy of the Word. Our 2,000 years of history, the teaching authority of the Church, our guidance by the Pope and his cardinal bishops, and our direct connection to the authority of the Apostles keep us united, regardless of where we happen to be.

How wonderful it is, Heavenly Father, that you have kept us united as your people in spite of endless attempts to break up the Catholic faith by those who would teach apostasy and heresy. I have one and a half billion brothers and sisters in every corner of the world. I know that many are having great difficulties, both in faith and in life. Offer comfort, blessings and support, please, my God, that they may survive both.

I-6 QUESTION: Sunday service with my non-Catholic friends seems more interesting than listening to the same old mass over and over. Why do we do that?

ANSWER: Wow! – you and I aren't watching the same mass! Yes, I know it can seem repetitive, but – with a little reflection – you might appreciate it a more.

Many faith expressions have good ideas about how to celebrate the Lord's Day, including great singing (which Catholics could be better at!), some intense preaching, some scripture, some singing … and a collection. Many of them offer or include some thoughtful bible study before or after service, and a whole lot of bonding through fellowship gatherings. None, though…NONE of them has the mass … at least not as we know and understand it. We are a church of smells, bells and miracles! Symbols of our faith abound!

Grab a good book about the meaning and symbolism within the

mass. We've got good resources locally for Catholic books – and, of course, the internet abounds with great books on Catholic liturgy. I can't completely cover the flow of our greatest liturgy, but here's a quick outline:

We enter, cleansing ourselves physically and calling our Baptism to mind by means of the holy water font and the sign of the cross, which itself reminds us to honor the three persons of the Trinity.

We gather as God's family, and become His body – the Church. When mass starts, we stop to examine how the week might have stained us, and ask for forgiveness – spiritual cleansing.

Soon the lector gets up to read from Scripture – first a selection from the Old Testament, related to the theme of today's Gospel. Then, we hear one of the Psalms, those great poetic, emotional readings, mostly from King David. A second reading is done, taken from the letters that circulated through the early Christian congregations to give them strength of faith. Now…an *Alleluia*! – rejoicing that the Gospel (the "good news") is coming, heard in the very words of Jesus, and we stand up to honor it. Then the homily.. usually themed to guide us into a better grasp of the ideas expressed in the scripture readings, followed by a recitation of the Nicene Creed. This creed (*credo*, I believe) condenses all of our basic beliefs into one prayer, and actually is used in most major Christian denominations. We remember now to find concern for others, in the Prayers of the Faithful. The first half of mass, the *Liturgy of the Word* is over – very similar to how Jesus would have celebrated *Shabbat* in the Temple and synagogues. So… now comes the *Liturgy of the Eucharist*, the second half of mass!

We send up our parish gifts of bread and wine to the altar, and the priest receives them. He washes his hands, representing a cleansing of all of us. Through the Eucharistic prayers that follow, our gifts are completely changed into the Body and Blood of Christ, (though the appearance stays). Through the priest and his ordination, standing in for Jesus – *in situ Christus* -the miracle first celebrated at the Last Supper continues to happen. Soon thereafter, we all stand and join in reciting the *Our Father* as a united assembly. Then Christ comes to us in Communion, in a real, physical presence. The very core of Catholic belief and celebration is right here, available to each of us.

After a pause to reflect and pray, we come quickly to the final prayers, some announcements, and the instruction from the priest or deacon: "The mass is finished! Go forth in peace to love one another"…..to carry the wonders of the mass through the coming week. And… the priest bestows a final blessing on all of us.

Mass, boring?! Nah, I don't think so!

I-7 Question: Why do Catholics need to go to church every Sunday, and even on some other days? I have a personal relationship with God, and I can talk to Him from wherever I happen to be on Sunday!

Answer: Jesus created a Church that is literally the Body of Christ – a family that currently numbers over a billion members. Yes, we're asked to "Keep holy the Lord's Day", and when we gather as family our prayers are multiplied and our faith renewed by community. Just as any family gains strength from getting together, sharing love and experiences – we gain strength from the Word of God and the Holy Eucharist celebrated with family in the wonderful liturgy of the Mass. How could we better spend the Sabbath than in unity with our brothers and sisters at our Father's table?

Lord, your mass is a wondrous celebration of your sacrifice, your creation, your glory. When I cannot attend for some serious reason I miss the experience tremendously. Keep my family and I in faith, that we may never lose the love we find for your people, especially in your church.

ABOUT THE AUTHOR

Who, me? I was raised in a solidly Catholic family, attended 12 years of Catholic schools, and took post-grad Christian Initiation courses at Loyola/Marymount University. I attended 3 years of Claretian seminary, a happy experience which changed my life, just at my antics there probably changed that of others. Still, my life has been spent, not as a priest, but as a family guy, and business owner. My experiences have brought me to who I am right now, right here. If any answers in this book are inaccurate or incomplete, they are solely my responsibility and/or opinions. I claim no vast expertise, simply a degree in *having-been-there*, having-done-that, and having thoroughly enjoyed the journey.

I live in Southern California, and attend Holy Name of Mary Catholic Parish in San Dimas, CA, where my wife and I are active in a variety of ministries.. Your comments or questions can be sent to: 178jerdar@gmail.com Thanks, and may God bless!